University of London Historical Studies

XVII

UNIVERSITY OF LONDON HISTORICAL STUDIES

I. HUGH TINKER. *The Foundations of Local Self-Government in India, Pakistan and Burma.* 1954

II. AVROM SALTMAN, *Theobald, Archbishop of Canterbury.* 1956

III. R. F. LESLIE. *Polish Politics and the Revolution of November 1830.* 1956

IV. W. N. MEDLICOTT. *Bismarck, Gladstone, and the Concert of Europe.* 1956

V. JOHN LYNCH. *Spanish Colonial Administration, 1782–1810: The Intendant System in the Viceroyalty of the Rio de la Plata.* 1958

VI. F. H. W. SHEPPARD. *Local Government in St. Marylebone, 1688–1835.* 1958

VII. R. L. GREAVES. *Persia and the Defence of India, 1884–1892.* 1959

VIII. M. J. SYDENHAM. *The Girondins.* 1961

IX. MARGARET HOWELL. *Regalian Right in Medieval England.* 1962

X. N. M. SUTHERLAND. *The French Secretaries of State in the Age of Catherine de Medici.* 1962

XI. GWYN A. WILLIAMS. *Medieval London: from Commune to Capital.* 1963

XII. CHARLES DUGGAN. *Twelfth-century Decretal Collections and their Importance in English History.* 1963

XIII. R. F. LESLIE. *Reform and Insurrection in Russian Poland 1856–65.* 1963

XIV. J. A. S. GRENVILLE. *Lord Salisbury and Foreign Policy.* 1964

XV. P. W. J. RILEY. *The English Ministers and Scotland, 1707–27.* 1964

XVI. J. F. BOSHER, *The Single Duty Project.* 1964

XVII. JOAN MCDONALD. *Rousseau and the French Revolution, 1762–1791.* 1965.

ROUSSEAU AND THE FRENCH REVOLUTION

1762–1791

Rousseau and the French Revolution 1762–1791

by

JOAN McDONALD

UNIVERSITY OF LONDON
THE ATHLONE PRESS
1965

Published by
THE ATHLONE PRESS
UNIVERSITY OF LONDON
at 2 Gower Street, London WC1
Distributed by Constable & Co Ltd
12 *Orange Street, London* WC2
Canada
Oxford University Press
Toronto
U.S.A.
Oxford University Press Inc
New York

Printed in Great Britain by
WILLIAM CLOWES AND SONS LTD
London and Beccles

PREFACE

THE purpose of this book is to determine the nature and extent of the political influence of Jean-Jacques Rousseau in France during the period 1762–1789 and in the first two years of the Revolution. Historians have too often been content to rely on what they regarded as similarities between Rousseau's theories and those of the revolutionaries. Moreover, in tracing the relationship between ideas and events there is a tendency to place too much emphasis on the supposed effect of the former on the latter, and to ignore the influence that events have on the later interpretation of a body of political theory. I have therefore tried to ignore traditional attributions of influence and to base this study first on an assessment of Rousseau's ideas seen in the context of his own times; and secondly, on an examination of the actual texts in which Rousseau's ideas were subsequently discussed by the revolutionary generation.

This work began as a thesis for the Degree of Doctor of Philosophy, approved by the University of London. Throughout its preparation I have been conscious of the help and cooperation I have received from many quarters. I would like to acknowledge particularly the assistance I received from the Central Research Fund of the University of London, and to express my appreciation of the friendly welcome given me by Westfield College as the recipient of one of its research awards. My thanks are due to Professor Alun Davies for his constructive criticism of the text and to Mr Peter Lindsay for his help in the correction of proofs. Above all, I would like to express my gratitude to Professor Alfred Cobban, whose constant interest and ready advice over many years have been invaluable.

J.McD.

CONTENTS

PART IV
Conclusion

ABBREVIATIONS

Works of Rousseau

Conf.	*Les Confessions de J. J. Rousseau*
C.G.P.	*Considérations sur le gouvernement de Pologne*
C.S.	*Contrat Social*
Corr. Gén.	*Correspondance Générale de J. J. Rousseau*, ed. T. Dufour, 1924–1934
D.G.	*Dédicace à la République de Genève* (contained in *D.I.*)
D.I.	*Discours sur l'origine et les fondements de l'inégalité parmi les hommes*
E.P.	*Discours sur l'Économie politique*
J.P.	*Jugement sur la Polysynodie*
L.M.	*Lettres écrites de la Montagne*
Œuvres	*Œuvres Complètes de J. J. Rousseau*, ed. L. S. Mercier, G. Brizzard, J. H. S. de l'Aulnaye, Paris, 1788

Other Abbreviations

Annales	*Annales de la Société Jean-Jacques Rousseau*, Geneva, 1905–
B.M.	British Museum
B.N.	Bibliothèque Nationale
L.A.	Librairie de l'Arsenal
Mon. Réimp.	*Réimpression de l'ancien Moniteur*, Paris, 1858
Vaughan	*The Political Writings of J. J. Rousseau*, ed. C. E. Vaughan, Cambridge, 1915

PART I

The Problem of Interpretation

CHAPTER I

Introduction: The Difficulties

SOME ideas are peculiar to an individual writer; others are general to a period of history. Ideas in action are more likely to belong to the second category than to the first, and this may be said of the ideas of the French Revolution. If we consider the ideas which were predominant in the minds of the early revolutionaries, we shall find that many streams of thought intermingled in them. They were derived, not from any one writer, but from a common pool of thought, from which both the revolutionaries and their opponents drew. Indeed, it is not what distinguishes a writer from his fellows that makes him influential, but rather what he has in common with them. If we consider Rousseau's works in relation to the philosophical background of the eighteenth century, we shall find that despite the distinguishing eccentricities of temperament and the originality of genius, he was a child of his own day, sharing in and contributing to its common beliefs.

It is difficult to isolate the thought of one writer from the general opinions of the day, and where Rousseau is concerned the task presents peculiar problems. Rousseau's name occupied a very particular place in revolutionary lore. He was regarded by the revolutionaries as their prophet and patron; his life was sometimes pictured as a martyrdom to the cause of the oncoming Revolution. He was described as the prototype of the man and citizen which the Revolution would produce. As we shall see, this revolutionary cult of Rousseau did not in fact originate in the study of Rousseau's political theory. Nevertheless, it gave rise to the assumption, on the part of the revolutionaries, that they were realizing in practice the ideals which had inspired Rousseau's writings. Hence on the one hand there was a tendency to pay tribute to Rousseau for a variety of revolutionary achievements, while on the other hand, revolutionary writers and speakers hoped to give added weight to their arguments by claiming Rousseau's authority. Thus his political influence may appear, at first sight, to have been greater during the Revolution than was in fact the case, and it is necessary to distinguish between the cult of Rousseau and the actual influence of his political thought.[1]

It is also necessary to bear in mind that the use of phrases such as 'the general will' or 'the inalienable sovereignty of the people', which are commonly associated with Rousseau, does not in itself necessarily establish that they are derived from the study, much less the acceptance of Rousseau's theories, even when these Rousseauist terms were used by writers who specifically appealed to his authority. The revolutionaries were seeking to realize in practice new forms of political organization, and their political phraseology, while providing an indication of the trend of ideas, provides little more. The use of a common political language does not necessarily imply either a unity of thought or a common familiarity with the sources of that language on the part of those who make daily use of it. Again, during a period of revolution there is a greater tendency to use theoretical and idealistic language, and old words may acquire new meanings in relation to novel political situations. The men of the French Revolution were themselves conscious of linguistic confusion. L. S. Mercier demanded a definition of all the principal political terms used in debate, so that the deputies in the National Assembly would have a common basis for discussion, and legislation would not depend on expressions the meanings of which were obscure.[2] During the period 1789–91 satirical dictionaries were popular, and aristocratic critics commented on the difference between the words used by the revolutionaries and the actual conditions of France which these words were intended to describe.

The use of revolutionary phraseology was, however, by no

[1] The revolutionary cult of Rousseau and its relation to the influence of Rousseau's political ideas are discussed more fully in Ch. XII.

[2] L. S. Mercier, *De J. J. Rousseau considéré comme l'un des premiers auteurs de la Révolution*, 1791, I, v, 70. It is only fair to say that Mercier himself contributed fairly generously to the confusion of which he complained.

means peculiar to revolutionary controversialists. Those who opposed the Revolution were brought up on the same intellectual food as those who supported it. Royal administrators had accepted in principle and had begun, in some cases, to realize in practice, many of the changes which the Revolution later brought about. Those strongholds of privilege, the Parlements, had from the middle of the century anticipated in their Remonstrances many of the arguments which the revolutionaries later used: for example, they based their claim to participate in legislation on the principle that the people were sovereign.[1] From 1788 onward the conservatives, consciously or unconsciously, made use of the same popular expressions as their rivals in order to make a bid for public support. The gap between language and intentions is perhaps nowhere better illustrated than in the famous *Mémoire sur les États Généraux*[2] of the Comte d'Antraigues, who used popular and apparently revolutionary phraseology to advocate a return to the medieval concept of monarchy and representation. Similarly we find that in the debates in the National Assembly on the royal veto, both the supporters of the veto and their opponents asserted that their object was to ensure the expression of the general will.[3]

While the adoption of new formulae in political controversy implies a general feeling that the old formulae are inadequate or irrelevant, and indicates broadly the new direction which society will take, such changes in thought do not proceed either quickly or evenly. In the first place, the older ways of thought do not die as rapidly as a change in phraseology may suggest; under an apparently revolutionary garb old ideas retain a tenacious life. Secondly, controversialists employ the popularly accepted phraseology in order to gain wider acceptance for their arguments. Hence, speeches and writings tricked

[1] See Ch. VII.

[2] E. L. H. de Launay d'Antraigues (Comte), *Mémoire sur les États Généraux, leurs droits et la manière de les convoquer*, 1788.

[3] *Mon. Réimp.*, 1789. The speeches of interest in this context are those of Mirabeau, on 1 September, A de Lameth, on 3rd, Mounier and de Sèze on 4th, and Malouet on 7th. The *Moniteur* for 1789, as is generally known, is not a contemporary account, but is a compilation dating from 1840 and drawn mainly from reports in the *Journal des Débats*, *Le Hodey* and the *Journal des deux Amis*. Malouet's speech was actually delivered on 1 September, and is wrongly dated in the *Moniteur*.

out in fashionable revolutionary jargon, and perhaps containing references to Rousseau's name or even quotations from his works, may reveal, on closer study, an astonishing variety of reasoning and conclusions hidden beneath the employment of identical political terms. It will be shown that Rousseau's name and his terms were used to justify monarchy and republicanism, constitutional government and direct democracy, and to gain a hearing for many of those bizarre individual panaceas which flourished in the hiatus between the collapse of traditional authority and the consolidation of new forms of government. Rousseau's name was used to support, and his phrases to express, policies which developed out of the practical circumstances of the Revolution, rather than out of his own theory. The use of phrases drawn from the *Social Contract* frequently indicates the influence of the Revolution on the interpretation of Rousseau, rather than the influence of Rousseau on the Revolution.

There are therefore objections to attempting to assess Rousseau's political influence on the basis of the frequency with which his name and his phraseology were used. It is necessary to go further, and to study in detail the use which revolutionary speakers and writers made of Rousseau's ideas before it is possible to assess how far these ideas were influential. This is not a simple task. Ideas are among the least stable elements in history, and the ideas of a great thinker, once expounded, are capable of development and variation in proportion to the needs of other human beings, though the same aspects will not necessarily appear relevant to different people or at different periods of time. Virginia Woolf wrote of Coleridge: 'When one takes a sentence of Coleridge into the mind, it explodes and gives birth to all kinds of other ideas, and that is the only sort of writing of which one can say that it has the secret of perpetual life.'[1] These words could equally well be applied to Rousseau. Indeed the same metaphor was used by Mercier in his study of Rousseau's works: 'Ce fut la capitale qui éveilla son génie: une question académique fut comme l'étincelle qui tomba sur le magasin de ses idées et causa l'explosion dont retentit le monde

[1] V. Woolf, *A Room of One's Own*, p. 84.

littéraire. . . .'[1] Rousseau's works and his personality have inspired a constant and continuing interest, and have given rise to extraordinarily divergent opinions. One may even regret the ease with which a philosophical corpse might be dissected, in comparison with the difficulties of pinning down the lively spirit of Rousseau's thought in the minds of men for whom the experience of revolution had heightened the powers of imagination.

Moreover, it would be unreal to expect an interpretation of Rousseau's ideas free from the bias of a variety of personal, social and political points of view, particularly during a revolution. Rousseau's political theory was discussed by writers of widely different viewpoints and each moulded the ideas of Rousseau to fit his own particular personal philosophy and political interests. For example, the aristocrat d'Antraigues wrote a romanticized history of traditional French government and found Rousseau's principles being applied in the relations between the medieval monarchy and Estates General.[2] The abbé Fauchet, on the other hand, made use of the *Social Contract* to further the cause of his mystical revolutionary internationalism.[3] Paul-Philippe Gudin, a constitutional monarchist, used Rousseau's theory of the general will as the basis for proposing a division of the legislative power into three branches.[4] L. S. Mercier and others used the *Social Contract* to support their arguments in favour of representation.[5] It is not always easy to decide how far such arguments were based on a genuine misunderstanding, and how far such writers consciously misused Rousseau's theories for their own purposes. Most human beings have a predilection for ideas which confirm the opinions they hold rather than for those which disturb them. Thus there can be a blending and blurring of ideas which in their original form were sharply defined and even contradictory.

Time is an equally, and perhaps even more important factor in the interpretation of a great man's work, for people's attitudes

[1] Mercier, I, i, 6.

[2] D'Antraigues, *Mémoire sur les États Généraux*, etc.

[3] See Ch. VI.

[4] P. P. Gudin, *Supplément au Contrat Social, applicable particulièrement aux grandes nations*, 1790, Ch. IV.

[5] Mercier. See Ch. VI.

to ideas are obviously affected by the experience of their own age, and those ideas which the eighteenth-century reader of Rousseau's works might fasten on to may not necessarily seem important to historians of the twentieth century. An outstanding example of a work which has come to assume a different significance with the passage of time is Rousseau's *Second Discourse.* When Rousseau wrote that society originated in the desire of the rich to fix for ever the laws of property and inequality, he was ringing a bell in the ear of the nineteenth and twentieth centuries, but not, it appears, in that of the eighteenth. When L. S. Mercier wanted to demonstrate that Rousseau was the precursor of the Revolution, and that the hatred of inequality was the mainspring of all his thought and writings, it was not to the *Discours sur l'Inégalité* that he turned, but to the *Émile* and the *Nouvelle Héloise,* in which Rousseau had attacked aristocratic privilege. Mercier regarded the *Second Discourse* simply as a theoretical *tour de force,* in which Rousseau satirized *la société policée.*[1] Similarly Mounier wrote that Rousseau's *Second Discourse* and Mably's *Discourse on the Natural Order of Societies* were 'in the estimation of the majority of readers considered merely as brilliant declamations, as pieces of wit, which did not call for a serious examination, and which excited no greater attention than did the "Utopia" of Sir Thomas More'.[2] Thus the historian must constantly guard against the temptation of reading into the minds of eighteenth-century men an interpretation of Rousseau's political theory which was only reached in the light of the experience of the nineteenth and twentieth centuries.

Further it must be remembered that living ideas undergo transmutation with changing conditions; like institutions they do not always continue to be important for the precise reasons which inspired their original inception. Motives and ends change with a changing social context. Thus a body of political theory ought to be seen in relation to the circumstances in which it arose, as well as in relation to what may be regarded as the subsequent logical development of the theory in relation

[1] Ibid. I, i, 18 and note.

[2] J. J. Mounier, *On the influence attributed to philosophers, freemasons, etc. on the Revolution of France,* pp. 39–40.

to a different situation. It is true that one cannot divide history into self-contained periods. At the same time, the study of the history of political thought indicates that ideas are not handed down from generation to generation in their logical entirety, but rather that each generation makes its own system of political theory, picking out ideas which seem relevant, and adapting others. We should be guilty of a serious distortion of Rousseau's theory if we considered it simply from the point of view of a search for the origins of the Revolution.[1]

Finally, in considering the influence of any political theorist on events it must be borne in mind that this study represents only one possible line of enquiry into the history of any period, and that there are many other factors which may perhaps be of equal or greater importance. The history of political thought is obviously important in itself, since it deals with what has been written about one of the most fundamental aspects of human life and relationships. Moreover the isolation of a certain factor in history for the purpose of detailed study is a prerequisite to the richer understanding of the whole. However, the process of tracing the emergence of a system of political theory and its development through a series of historical situations may lead to the placing of undue emphasis upon a purely logical and intellectual reaction to events. In practice, of course, human behaviour is affected by a variety of factors. In the urgent crisis of a revolution governments may fall back on traditional methods. The actual number of courses of action open to them at any moment will be limited. They may act according to theory, or, having acted, they may explain and justify their actions in terms of those political and social theories which are familiar to them, and to whose authority they can with advantage appeal. The relation of such theories to the events is not, of course, accidental, for it is the character of the great thinker to sum up ideas and tendencies which, previously inarticulate or inadequately expressed, nevertheless have their roots in the realities of the social situation, and which, therefore, are likely to produce, sooner or later, their practical repercussions. The generic association between theory and practice is to be found

[1] Compare D. Mornet, *Les Origines intellectuelles de la Révolution française*, 1933, Conclusions, p. 471.

in the conditions of society which gives rise to both, rather than in the genesis of the events from the theory. At the same time, contemporaries see events through the eyes of those theorists with whose writings they are familiar, and those writings assume, as a result, a new significance to them.

Rousseau summed up in his writings much that was deeply felt by his contemporaries, but we must ask ourselves whether, in the political sphere, the question of his influence, and the interpretation of his works would have been regarded as important had not the Revolution provided the opportunities for attacking in practice those abuses which Rousseau had attacked in theory. Mounier, seeking to assess the importance of the ideas of the eighteenth-century philosophers on the events of 1789 concluded: 'It was not the influence of those principles which created the Revolution, it was on the contrary the Revolution which created their influence.'[1]

[1] Mounier, p. 108.

CHAPTER II

Earlier Historical Interpretations

1. The Variety of Historical Judgement

HISTORIANS have reached a variety of conclusions about the role of Rousseau's political theory before and during the Revolution. Meynier,[1] Fabre,[2] Chuquot[3] and de Maday[4] have seen in Rousseau the liberal champion of the theory of the contract and of individual rights, whose ideas were given expression during 1789–91 by the Constituent Assembly. They regarded the *Social Contract* as the most influential of Rousseau's works, though Meynier thought that the Girondins were influenced by the *Nouvelle Héloise* and André de Maday argued that the *Émile*, the *Second Discourse* and the *Discours sur l'Économie Politique* were also important. Louis Blanc distinguished between two separate phases of the Revolution. The first was the revolt of the bourgeoisie against the aristocracy, for which he believed Voltaire to have been responsible; the second was the revolution of the people against the bourgeoisie, which he regarded as having originated in the works of Rousseau. He regarded the *Second Discourse* as the most influential of Rousseau's works, containing as it did, the attack on property.[5]

Jules Lemaître disapproved equally of Rousseau and the Revolution, and blamed him for all that he regarded as its worst features. He regarded the *Social Contract* as Rousseau's

[1] A. Meynier, *J. J. Rousseau, révolutionnaire*, 1911.
[2] Joseph Fabre, *Jean-Jacques Rousseau*, 1912.
[3] A. Chuquot, *Jean-Jacques Rousseau*, 1906.
[4] A. de Maday, 'Rousseau et la Révolution', 1937. *Annales*, 1938, XXI.
[5] Louis Blanc, *Histoire de la Révolution française*, 1862.

most influential work.[1] Edgar Quinet rather fancifully identified different phases of the Revolution with different works by Rousseau, beginning with the *Émile* and working through to the *Dialogues*. He asserted: 'La Révolution se modèle sur lui; à mesure qu'elle développe, elle semble une incarnation de Jean-Jacques.'[2] Edmé Champion, on the other hand, denied that Rousseau's influence was as great as had generally been supposed. He considered that it was at its height during the period 1789–91, but that the association of Rousseau's name with the idea of constitutional monarchy resulted in the eclipse of his prestige after Varennes.[3] Professor David Williams came to the directly contrary conclusion that Rousseau's influence was negligible during the years 1789–92, but that it 'came into its own' with the ascendancy of Robespierre.[4] Finally, and more recently, Professor Talmon has argued that all those elements of totalitarianism which emerged during the Revolution, from 1789 onward, originated in and were derived from the *Social Contract*.[5]

Among the historians referred to above, Edmé Champion alone based his conclusions on a detailed study of individual interpretations of Rousseau's theories. He examined the opinions of men and women of a variety of personal, social and political viewpoints, as expressed in speeches, memoirs and histories composed before, during and after the Revolution. The same method was followed by David Williams, but less thoroughly and in a more limited study. More recently, Professor McNeil has contributed two detailed studies of particular aspects of the Revolution, which have done much to clarify the character of Rousseau's influence. The first, a study of the Rousseauist cult during the Revolution, has indicated that a distinction must be made between the great prestige in which Rousseau's name was held on the one hand, and the actual extent of his political influence on the other. The second, pub-

[1] Jules Lemaître, *Jean-Jacques Rousseau*, 1909. The quotations in the text are taken from the English edition of 1910.

[2] Edgar Quinet, *La Révolution*, 1866.

[3] E. Champion, *Rousseau et la Révolution française*, 1909.

[4] D. Williams, 'The influence of Rousseau on political opinion, 1760–95', *English Historical Review*, XLVIII (1933), pp. 414–30.

[5] J. L. Talmon, *The Origins of Totalitarian Democracy*, 1952.

lished soon after the completion of Part III of this work, is a discussion of the degree to which the critics of the Revolution appealed to the authority of Rousseau.[1]

In the main, the case for Rousseau's influence has been argued by the selection of parallels, by the comparison, that is, between Rousseau's theories on the one hand, and the events and ideas of the Revolution on the other. Instead of enquiring into the extent and nature of Rousseau's influence, historians have been content to take this influence for granted and have differed only in their estimates of which particular ideas were regarded as important and by which particular Revolutionary groups. In order to illustrate this method more clearly it is proposed to examine in greater detail some of their interpretations.

2. Jules Lemaître (1909)

Lemaître levelled a universal condemnation against Rousseau for all the worst excesses of the French Revolution. His method was to project the theories of the *Social Contract*, as he interpreted them, into the Revolution, and to rely on kindling the imagination of his readers in order to win acceptance for his arguments. The fact that his study of Rousseau began life as a series of lectures may account in part for his rhetorical style. A few extracts illustrate his method of argument. For example, his verdict on the influence exercised by the last chapter of the *Social Contract*, on the civil religion, runs as follows:

> When one remembers that the dogmas in question besides the sanctity of God and the future life, comprise the sanctity of the Social Contract and of the laws, one seems to hear the clauses of the sentence which, thirty years later, were to send so many people—among them Malesherbes, André Chenier and Lavoisier—to the guillotine. . . . [2]

[1] Gordon McNeil, 'The Cult of Rousseau and the French Revolution', *Journal of the History of Ideas*, VI (1945), pp. 197–212, and also 'The Anti-Revolutionary Rousseau', *American Historical Review*, LVIII (1952–3), pp. 808–23.

[2] Lemaître, *Jean-Jacques Rousseau*, pp. 262–3.

Similarly, describing Rousseau's theory of the Tribunate (in Book IV, Ch. v), he asked:

Do you not already see rising before you all the machinery of government during the Terror?[1]

Lemaître acknowledged that Rousseau would not, in fact, have approved of this application of his theories, but he gave him little credit for this.

Never, I believe, thanks to human credulity and stupidity, has a writer done more than this writer, who, it seems, did not exactly know what he was saying: he would besides have fled from his city, had it been what he dreamed. Really, there are times when one is tempted to say that this wretched man was a criminal.[2]

Nor did Lemaître give much credit to the intelligence of the revolutionaries, who in his view swallowed the *Social Contract* whole, and tried to apply its maxims to France regardless of practical considerations.

The form of government which the author described as fit only for a city of 20,000 souls . . . (and that later he acknowledged to be impossible even in so small a city, and finally disowned with a kind of fury), the Revolution, thirty years later will adopt like a gospel, seeking to impose it on a people ten centuries old, and with a population of 28 millions. And this venture will be called the reign of terror. . . . All the most stupid and murderous prejudices of the Revolution came from the Social Contract.[3]

When Lemaître came to consider how these 'stupid and murderous prejudices' were disseminated, he put forward only one piece of evidence. He repeated Mallet du Pan's account of Marat reading and commenting on the *Social Contract* to the applause of enthusiastic audiences in public squares, a scene which Mallet claimed to have witnessed in 1788.[4] From this Lemaître concluded:

[1] Ibid. p. 264. [2] Ibid. p. 278. [3] Ibid. p. 278.

[4] See the *Mercure Britannique*, 10 March 1799, II, No. xiv, 'Du degré d'influence qu'a eu la philosophie française sur la Révolution'. Mallet stated: 'J'ai entendu, en 1788, Marat lire et commenter le Contrat Social dans les promenades publiques, aux applaudissements d'un auditoire enthousiaste. J'aurais peine à citer un seul Révolutionnaire qui ne fût transporté de ces théorèmes anarchiques et qui ne brûlât du désir de les réaliser. Ce Contrat Social qui dissout la société fut le Coran des discoureurs apprêtés de 1789, des Jacobins de 1790, des Républicains de 1791, et des forcenés les plus atroces.'

And five years later France tasted the benefits of the Social Contract doctrines, and of universal equality, of the people's sovereignty, and the absolute rights of the state, of the exceptional magistracy such as the Committee of Public Safety, and the revolutionary tribunal. From Chapter VIII of Book IV came the anti-Catholic prejudices, the civil constitution of the clergy, and religious persecution. And the Social Contract took the shape of law in the inapplicable constitution of 1793. All that, because, thirty years before, a half demented man took it into his head to imagine for a society of 20,000 inhabitants a legislation which was 'fit only for gods'—and to which, five years later, he declared the most arbitrary despotism to be preferable.[1]

Finally, Lemaître asserted:

Without him, without some phrases of this stranger, in his Discourse on Inequality, especially without his Social Contract, it is possible that in 1792 no one would have thought of proclaiming the Republic.[2]

3. Albert Meynier (1912)

Unlike Lemaître, Meynier approved of Rousseau, whom he regarded as a champion of liberal parliamentarianism, drawing attention to the likenesses which he perceived between the theory of the *Social Contract* and the practical achievements of the Constituent Assembly. He concluded that these likenesses were proof of the influence of Rousseau's political theory. He argued that at different times during the Revolution, different groups or individuals were influenced by different works of Rousseau, and even by different parts of the same work. The members of the Constituent Assembly he regarded as having been the interpreters of the first three books of the *Social Contract*. Robespierre, he believed, had tried to apply the principles of Book IV. The Girondins he regarded as being the products of the *Nouvelle Héloise*; Mme. Roland he entitled 'Julie révolutionnaire'. Buzot was identified with Saint-Preux, Roland with Wolmar. Meynier also distinguished between what he regarded as the correct interpretation of Rousseau's political thought and

[1] Lemaître, *Jean-Jacques Rousseau*, p. 278.
[2] Ibid. p. 355. Compare p. 346.

what he regarded as erroneous. For example he praised the men of 1789–91 for having correctly understood Rousseau's theory, and for having applied it in the Declaration of Rights and the constitution of 1791. On the other hand he rebuked Robespierre for inaugurating the Terror, and for confusing the civil and religious powers, which he believed was a further development of what had already been an unfortunate mistake on the part of the author of the *Social Contract*. Thus, in Meynier's view, Rousseau deserved praise for the liberal policy of 1789–91, but blame for the law of Prairial, and we find him classifying the *Social Contract* as good and bad in parts, according to what he believed the revolutionaries subsequently made of it, and without at any point seriously examining the evidence for its influence.[1]

4. André de Maday (1937)

Like both Lemaître and Meynier, André de Maday did not question the importance of Rousseau's influence during the Revolution, in view, as he said, of the great weight of historical evidence on this subject. The works of Rousseau which might have been regarded as important by the revolutionaries were, he declared, the *Social Contract*, the *Second Discourse*, the *Discours sur l'Économie Politique* and the *Considérations sur le gouvernement de Pologne*. He then picked out what he called the three *doctrines maîtresses* of Rousseau's philosophy, which he believed the revolutionaries would obviously have regarded as important. These were: the condemnation of the Ancien Régime; the theory of the contract, including the principles of popular sovereignty and democracy; and the postulates of liberty and equality. Thus he began by assuming the conclusions which could justifiably have been reached only at the end of his study.

His method of showing how the influence of Rousseau's political theory could be recognized is illustrated by the chain of reasoning by which he proved, to his own satisfaction, that Rousseau inspired the taking of the Bastille. In the *Second Discourse*, he argued, Rousseau stated that liberty was the noblest

[1] Meynier, *J. J. Rousseau, révolutionnaire*, p. 77.

faculty of man. The taking of the Bastille was the victory of liberty, and the proof that it was due to Rousseau is provided by the fact that his bust was made out of the stones of the Bastille, with the inscription of the Rights of Men round the base. 'C'est donc la manifestation de l'opinion publique révolutionnaire qui a attribué à Rousseau la paternité spirituelle de la prise de la Bastille!'[1]

By a similar process of reasoning Rousseau was credited with the Oath of the Tennis Court, the events of the night of 4th August, and the Declaration of Rights.

De Maday, however, regarded Rousseau's theory as contributing only to what he regarded as best in the Revolution. Hence he opposed the arguments of Lemaître, and asserted that the Terror was due to a misunderstanding, on Robespierre's part, of the *Social Contract*, for which Rousseau himself could not be held responsible.

5. J. L. Talmon (1952)

More important from the point of view of this study are the views of Professor Talmon, who argues, in his book *The Origins of Totalitarian Democracy* that in the *Social Contract* can be discovered the germs of modern mass democracy, the classless society, dictatorship and the monolithic state. He asserts that in marrying the concept of the general will with the principle of popular sovereignty, Rousseau gave rise to totalitarian democracy.[2] He argues that Rousseau's theory of the general will is essentially totalitarian and that the revolutionary theory of the general will was the same as, and indeed derived from, that stated in the *Social Contract*. In the years leading up to 1789, ideas, according to Talmon, acquired a new importance as 'historic agents'. Tradition, he writes, was replaced by abstract reason. 'The ideologist', he asserts, 'came to the fore'. Among the ideologists who influenced the French people before and during the Revolution, he regards Rousseau as holding a preeminent position. Sieyès he regards as the first important practical exponent of Rousseauism. During the period 1789 to 1791

[1] A. de Maday, 'Rousseau et la Révolution', p. 196.

[2] Talmon, *Origins*, p. 43.

Sieyès was, in Talmon's view, 'the chief spokesman of the Revolution' and he describes him as 'interpreting Rousseau'. For Sieyès, he argues, the National Assembly, was 'not just a representative body, but Rousseau's people in assembly really'.[1] But Rousseau's theories were carried to their logical conclusion by Robespierre and Saint-Just and finally by Babeuf.

It is possible to make some general criticisms of the methods used by the four historians discussed above. Three of them explicitly deny the necessity of trying to trace the channels by which Rousseau's influence reached the revolutionaries as a means of assessing the degree and nature of that influence. Meynier held such a study to be superfluous. De Maday asserted that 'en présence de l'identité de la doctrine de Rousseau exposée dans le Contrat Social et de l'œuvre politique de la Révolution, l'influence de Rousseau est indéniable'.[2] Talmon takes the same view.

> Statistics [he writes], have been adduced to show that the works of the philosophers were neither widely distributed nor widely read in the years before the Revolution. . . . On becoming acquainted with the Revolutionary literature one is almost tempted to answer that statistics are no science. The prevalence of philosophical canon books in libraries or the number of their actual readers is in reality no index of their influence.

He then goes on to point out that 'there is such a thing as a climate of ideas, as ideas in the air'.[3] It is, however, precisely the difficulty of distinguishing between the climate of opinion and the influence of one particular writer which this method of comparison ignores. Unless it is possible to show that the theories under consideration have actually been derived from the text of the *Social Contract*, what evidence is there that they were not drawn from that common fund of ideas to which so many eighteenth-century writers contributed? The three 'doctrines maîtresses' of the Revolution picked out by de Maday as deriving specifically from the political theory of Rousseau are

[1] Talmon, *Origins*, pp. 69–75.
[2] A de Maday, 'Rousseau et la Révolution', p. 107.
[3] Talmon, *Origins*, pp. 69–70.

precisely those general ideas in the formulation of which it is impossible to discern the influence of one thinker more than that of another. It is impossible to claim that the idea of the contract, or the sovereignty of the people, or the ideals of liberty and equality were peculiar to the writings of Rousseau. Similarly it is impossible to accept Meynier's argument that the Declaration of Rights was derived directly from the *Social Contract*, or to accept his view that the very concept of a Declaration of Rights bears the peculiar stamp of Rousseau's thought. Meynier argued that the revolutionaries were emulating Rousseau's philosophical method by relating the ends of political power to certain universal principles.[1] As Professor Derathé has pointed out, however, the abstract treatment of political questions, and the deduction of constitutional rights from fundamental principles, was the method followed by all the political theorists of the eighteenth century, only excepting Montesquieu.[2] To assume that the revolutionaries were following Rousseau in this instance is to divorce both the Revolution and the writings of Rousseau from their common historical context. All political power is justified according to certain principles, and it is the work of revolutionaries to re-define these principles —they would not be revolutionaries if they did not—and it was the need for a re-definition of the ends of political power which produced both the *Social Contract* and the events of 1789.

The method of relying on parallels between revolutionary and Rousseauist theory inevitably leads to the over-emphasis of one factor in a complicated historical situation. In answer to Meynier, it is possible to point out that the idea of individual rights was general during the eighteenth century. In reply to Talmon it is possible to argue that Sieyès did not have to read Rousseau's condemnation of 'partial associations' in order to condemn aristocratic privilege. Neither Robespierre nor any other child of the eighteenth century needed to read the *Social Contract* to become acquainted with the idea of absolute state authority.[3] And it is perhaps not extravagant to maintain that

[1] Meynier, *J. J. Rousseau, révolutionnaire*, pp. 80–1.

[2] R. Derathé, *Rousseau et la science politique de son temps*, 1950, pp. 23–4.

[3] Not only Talmon, but also Faguet, in his book *Rousseau, penseur*, 1910, argued that Rousseau's political theory left the individual defenceless against the state; see p. 406 ff.

the Bastille might still have been taken even if the *Social Contract* had never been written.

To select ideas from the *Social Contract*, or from other works of Rousseau, and then compare these ideas with those expressed during the Revolution, as a means of establishing the influence of Rousseau's theories, is to take for granted precisely what the argument is purporting to prove. How the revolutionaries thought about Rousseau can only be discovered by studying what they themselves said and wrote about him. The failure to examine such evidence inevitably involves an arbitrary and subjective choice of parallels. If the historian assumes that certain ideas in the *Social Contract* were regarded as important by the revolutionaries, and then looks for evidence of the expression of the same or similar ideas during the Revolution, then the possibility that the revolutionaries may have interpreted Rousseau's theories differently is overlooked. For instance, Talmon writes of Saint-Just that in asserting, in 1791, that monarchy was the best form of government for large states, he was following in the best traditions of Montesquieu.[1] Rousseau also emphasized this point in the *Social Contract*, and many writers in the early years of the Revolution quoted from the *Social Contract* in support of monarchy. Talmon, however, has already labelled Rousseau as the first great protagonist of totalitarian democracy, and has set out to show that the revolutionaries derived their totalitarian concepts from the *Social Contract*. It would therefore weaken his argument if he drew attention to the fact that Rousseau was a supporter of the traditional monarchical form of government, or to the fact that he was frequently quoted as such during the Revolution.

Similarly, Meynier, who quoted L. S. Mercier's book as evidence of Rousseau's influence, rejected the work of the aristocrat Lenormant as evidence of a different interpretation of Rousseau's theory during the Revolution. He dismissed Lenormant's lengthy pamphlet as of no importance on the ground that the author had quoted not from the *Social Contract*, which had been the inspiration of the Constituent Assembly, but from the *Considérations sur le gouvernement de Pologne*. In fact,

[1] Talmon, *Origins*, p. 88.

Lenormant quoted widely from many of Rousseau's works, and was more accurate in his discussion of Rousseau's texts than Mercier. Out of a total of sixty-nine references and quotations from Rousseau's works, twenty-nine were taken from the *Social Contract* and twenty-two from the *Considérations*. Lenormant's pamphlet was moreover only one among many which based a condemnation of the work of the National Assembly on Rousseau's theory in general and the *Social Contract* in particular, and which Meynier ignored.[1] Both Meynier and de Maday lay much stress on the fact that the revolutionaries themselves claimed to be acting as disciples of Rousseau, but such claims may be evidence of the prestige attached to Rousseau's name rather than of anything more.

It is of course possible to disprove the influence of Rousseau by the methods that are commonly used to prove it. Cahen, in an article of 1912,[2] criticized Meynier's argument for the influence of the *Social Contract* between 1789 and 1791 on the ground that the whole concept of a Declaration of Rights was in fundamental disagreement with Rousseau's theories, and that the Constitution of 1791 bore no resemblance to the ideas contained in the *Social Contract*. But to disprove Rousseau's influence on the basis of the unlikeness of the work of the revolutionaries and the theory of the *Social Contract* is simply to reverse the application of the method which I have already criticized. To assert that the revolutionary ideas are unlike those of Rousseau is not to prove that the revolutionaries were uninfluenced by Rousseau's theories, any more than to argue that they are alike is to prove that they were influenced by them.

Two important points emerge from the consideration of previous studies: in the first place, one must not begin with an assumption of identity between the ideas of Rousseau and those of the Revolution; in the second, one must study what the revolutionaries themselves wrote and said, instead of beginning with a preconceived view and then looking for examples with which to bolster it up.

[1] C. F. Lenormant, *Jean-Jacques Rousseau, aristocrate*, 1790. For a fuller discussion of this and other aristocratic pamphlets dealing with Rousseau's political theory, see Part III below.

[2] L. Cahen, 'Rousseau et la Révolution française', *Revue de Paris* (1912), Année XIX.

CHAPTER III

Rousseau and the Revolutionary State

I. Was Rousseau a Revolutionary?

One assumption on which the interpretation of Rousseau's influence on the Revolution is usually based is the supposition that in the *Social Contract* and elsewhere, he showed himself as an advocate of revolution.[1] It may be argued that the intentions of an author are not important in the assessment of the influence of his ideas. It is certainly true that the ideas of a political philosopher almost inevitably become distorted in the process of their dissemination to a wider public. Some ideas are taken out of their context and overemphasized at the expense of the whole. Neither men of action nor hungry crowds are interested in the subtleties which occupy the mind of the philosopher. Ideas are understood at different levels, and the theories of the philosopher must be simplified and streamlined by politicians if they are to be used as popular slogans. For this very reason a distinction must be made between the theory of the philosopher and the subsequent interpretation of his work. Unless this is done both the theory and the interpretation will be misunderstood. If no account is taken of Rousseau's own intentions, and if his theories are

[1] The most recent example of this assumption is to be found in J. Bronowski and Bruce Mazlish, *The Western Intellectual Tradition*, 1960. In chapter xvi, pp. 280–304, Rousseau is described as a revolutionary thinker producing the 'slogans' of 'democratic and totalitarian government'. On p. 299 it is suggested that in practical politics the idea of the general will is capable only of a 'totalitarian interpretation'. Rousseau, it is asserted, on p. 303, 'planted the seeds which flourished in the Revolution of 1789, the reign of Robespierre and the dictatorship of Napoleon'. It is generally implied that Rousseau's theories were decisive in influencing events during the Revolution and the Napoleonic period. See, for example, chapter xxii, pp. 402–403.

judged only in terms of their various interpretations, what is peculiar in Rousseau's political thought is lost, and his theories are swallowed up in a vague and arbitrarily defined 'Rousseauism'. Thus, for the historians Meynier and de Maday, 'Rousseauism' meant liberty, legal equality, and constitutional government. For Lemaître it was absolutism and persecution. For Talmon, 'Rousseauism' is the prologue to modern left-wing totalitarianism, though in a note to his text, he argues that Rousseau's theories also had their place in the development of a totalitarianism of the right, by way of the theories of Fichte, Hegel and Savigny.[1] What Rousseau wrote, however, is quite distinct from what either the constitutional monarchists of 1789, or Robespierre, or the modern dictators of both the right and the left have written or said or done.

Admittedly, it is difficult for the reader of Rousseau's political theory not to go somewhat further than he himself was prepared to go. In his discussion of popular sovereignty, Rousseau explored in theory a concept with which later generations were to become preoccupied in practice. Thus there is always the danger of reading back into Rousseau's work rather more than is justified if we are not to divorce him from his eighteenth-century context, and to attribute to him ideas which may be hinted at in his writings but for the later development of which he can hardly be held responsible. Moreover, Rousseau's eloquence and the burning passion of his style are liable to obscure his own views as to what was practically possible; the reader may be carried along at such a pace that in the end he goes crashing through the barriers of caution which Rousseau himself erected, without even noticing that they were there. Thus the *Social Contract* may easily mislead the reader, for although Rousseau's conservatism is implicit, his subject and treatment give it the appearance of a revolutionary work.

Rousseau was concerned to establish the principles of political right. Like Plato, he uncovered the fundamental roots of society in the course of his search for 'Justice'. No one has nailed *The Republic* to a revolutionary mast, and it is difficult to argue that Rousseau, any more than Plato, visualized his work as a programme for revolutionary action, or indeed for any

[1] Talmon, *Origins*, p. 280.

action at all. The abstract character of the work is well within the traditions of eighteenth-century speculative philosophy. Rousseau himself pointed this out in the *Lettres écrites de la Montagne* when he claimed that he merely followed what was the common pattern in political philosophy:

Locke, Montesquieu, l'abbé de Saint-Pierre ont traité les mêmes matières et souvent avec la même liberté tout au moins. . . .Tous sont nés sous les rois, ont vécu tranquilles, et sont morts honorés dans leurs pays.[1]

The foreword for the *Social Contract* suggests that Rousseau did not expect it to have much effect except as a purely theoretical and speculative essay.

There are, of course, important differences between Rousseau's political theory and that of his immediate predecessors. He wrote in an age and a country which, dissatisfied with the application and philosophical basis of political power, had come to believe that political institutions could become the instruments for the progressive amelioration of man's lot by the utilization of new knowledge, and under the guidance of human reason. The consideration of political justice was, in fact, no longer an abstract philosophical pursuit; political theory was being projected into the new sphere of practical sociology. Before the *Social Contract* was written, Montesquieu had demonstrated the method of fact-collecting as the basis for a study of society in all its aspects. Rousseau himself was affected by the empiricism of his age. In the *Social Contract* he attempted to combine the abstract consideration of political principles with observation on actual political systems. At the same time he wrote in a style which betrayed his passionate conviction of the corruption of existing social institutions. Thus the *Social Contract* has a disturbing dualism. G. D. H. Cole wrote of Rousseau's method:

His general remarks had such a way of bearing very obvious particular application, and were so obviously inspired by a particular attitude towards the governments of his day, that even philosophy became in his hands unsafe, and he was attacked for what men read between the lines of his works. It is owing to this faculty

[1] *L.M.*, let. vi; Vaughan, II, 206.

for giving his generalisations content and actuality that Rousseau has become the father of modern political philosophy. He uses the method of his time only to transcend it; out of the abstract and the general he creates the concrete and universal.[1]

Rousseau himself was aware of this quality of his work. Although he compared his political theory with that of Locke, Montesquieu and Saint-Pierre, he put his finger on the point of difference between his own work and that of the eighteenth-century philosophers, when he wrote:

Eh! monsieur, si je n'avais fait qu'un système, vous êtes bien sûr qu'on n'aurait rien dit: on se fût contenté de reléguer le Contrat social avec la République de Platon, l'Utopie et les Sévarambes, dans le pays des chimères. Mais je peignais un objet existant, et l'on voulait que cet objet changeât de face. Mon livre portait témoignage contre l'attentat qu'on allait faire: voilà ce qu'on ne m'a pas pardonné.[2]

The *Social Contract* lends itself to the diverse interpretations which, as will be shown, are to be found in the revolutionary pamphlets because continuously and almost imperceptibly Rousseau changed his ground, arguing now from principles, now from facts, so that it is not always immediately possible to distinguish between what he puts forward as his ideal and what merely as a probable consequence of actual facts. Moreover, since he admitted that institutions which in themselves might be undesirable might at the same time be inevitable in certain circumstances, he could be interpreted as advocating in practice institutions which in theory he condemned. Thus Rousseau could be quoted by writers during the Revolution as having advocated or condemned monarchy, or intermediate bodies, according to where the particular writer took his stand, for while Rousseau rejected monarchy and intermediate bodies as incompatible with the expression of the general will, he also regarded them as necessary parts of the government of large states.

Finally, it is necessary to remember that when Rousseau put forward the theory of inalienable popular sovereignty he

[1] G. D. H. Cole, *The Social Contract and Discourses of J. J. Rousseau*, 1941. Introduction, p. ix.

[2] *L.M.*, let. vi, Vaughan, II, 203.

visualized his ideal society in the guise of the ancient city state. Fundamentally he was more conservative than those exponents of enlightened despotism who believed that the power of the state could be used for the progressive amelioration of society. Rousseau had little belief in the possibility of human progress. On the contrary, his view of society was essentially the Platonic one of a continuous falling away from the ideal. The older the society, the less was it likely to give realization to those potentialities of human virtue which it was within the powers of a young society to develop. Moreover, Rousseau did not believe that the process of degeneration could be arrested or reversed. The writer whose name was above all associated with the idea of 'regeneration' during the Revolution denied that the regeneration of states was possible except on very rare occasions, and repeatedly emphasized in the *Social Contract* and elsewhere, the dangers which accompany any disturbance of the traditional ways of life and government.[1]

In practice Rousseau pinned his faith on the traditional morality of society preserved in custom. Hence his preference for rural society, which is conservative, as opposed to life in the towns, where custom tends to break down. In the *Dédicace* to the *Second Discourse* he expressed this thankfulness that he did not live in the tempestuous conditions of a new society,[2] and in his comments on the proposals of the abbé de Saint-Pierre, he asked who would be prepared to take it upon himself to abolish old customs, even if the advantages of the new plan of reform were incontestable.[3] Rousseau even rejected the eighteenth century's panacea for human betterment, the increase and diffusion of enlightenment. He held that increased knowledge would not solve human problems. His educational theories were based on the principle that man should learn those things which were within the range of his sense perceptions at the rate which was natural to the growth of his needs, and that he should learn only what was directly useful and natural to him. Unlike Helvétius, Rousseau accepted the influence of environment only as complementary to the innate potentialities of the indi-

[1] *C.S.*, II, ch. viii; Vaughan, II, 55–6.
[2] *D.G.*, *D.I.*, Vaughan, I, 126.
[3] *J.P.*, Vaughan, I, 416.

vidual. Therefore he did not sacrifice the essential nature of man to the possibility of perfection by regarding him as clay to be moulded by the educationist. As Becker pointed out, the innate ideas which Locke had so politely dismissed through the hall door, Rousseau brought back through the kitchen window.[1] The idea of the innate nature of man was the central point of Rousseau's political, educational and romantic works. Man developed as a moral being under the dual guidance of nature and society. Society was good in so far as it afforded him the opportunity for attaining a higher moral and rational existence in harmony with his innate potentialities. In the customs of society human morality was both expressed and created. 'Le moindre changement dans les coutumes, fût-il même avantageux à certains égards, tourne toujours au préjudice des mœurs.'[2]

Thus in Rousseau's view one might seek the true principles which would allow for the social development of man according to his nature, instead of in violation of it, but the possibility of those principles being realized in practice was dependent on factors largely outside human control. The age of a society, its size, its geographical and physical character, the wealth or povery of its people, determined its institutions. In Rousseau's thought the gap between the ideal and reality is so great that one feels that either his pessimism was the result of the standard of perfection demanded by the remorseless logic of his theory, or else his idealism was the reverse side of his practical disillusionment and a religion of despair.

2. Was Rousseau the Precursor of the Totalitarian State?

How far can it be argued that Rousseau's theory of the general will is totalitarian? The charges made against Rousseau are twofold. Firstly, he insisted that the general will could not be expressed by representatives. It is argued that an attempt to apply this theory would lead to direct democracy, and that

[1] Carl Becker, *The Heavenly City of the Eighteenth Century Philosophers*, 1932, p. 87.
[2] *Œuvres*, VIII, *Narcisse*, Préface, p. xxiv.

such a system would in turn lead inevitably to dictatorship. Secondly, it is argued that by insisting that the general will was the expression of man's higher self, Rousseau opened the way to a new form of dictatorship. Men could now be forced along a course dictated to them by their rulers in defiance of their expressed will, because their rulers could claim to be acting in accordance with their real will. If, moreover, it is accepted that for the general will to be expressed it is necessary to reach unanimity on all political issues, then in practice the state must be to a high degree coercive, and must be active in educating the citizen to will correctly. The individual must be subjected to constant pressure throughout his life, must be absorbed in communal activities and submitted to emotional and highly organized demonstrations of unity which allow him no opportunity to think for himself. Since what Rousseau called the 'private and personal loyalties' are the greatest enemies to social unanimity there must be a progressive elimination of all individual differences and inequalities. Hence it is argued that from Rousseau's theory of the general will stem dictatorship, collectivism and ultimately communism.

The function of the legislator in the *Social Contract* has been compared with that of the modern revolutionary dictator, and the 'general will' has been identified with 'the party line'. During a revolution, it is argued, those who rise against the established laws and institutions claim that they express the real will of the nation. In fact, however, it is not the people who become the legislators, but their leaders. These men act on behalf of the nation, and they use their power to prepare for the people what they, as their leaders, believe is best for them. This involves the elimination of those individuals who do not conform and the re-education of what is left by all those forms of pressure and mass stimulation familiar to the student of modern totalitarian societies.[1]

This linking of Rousseau's theory with nineteenth- and twentieth-century developments is open to criticism. Tyrannies are a form of government well known to historians of every era. They have their genesis in the reaction of societies to circumstances, and as far as modern tyrannies are concerned, it seems

[1] See Talmon, *Origins*, p. 47.

reasonable to assume that they would have taken much the same form had Rousseau never expounded his theory of the general will.

If we are to understand Rousseau's concept of the general will it is essential that we should consider his ideas not in relation to events which he could not possibly have foreseen, but against the background of his own times and the evils which he was attacking. When we speak of Rousseau's theories 'involving' or 'implying' this or that inevitable consequence, we must bear in mind that they did not necessarily 'involve' or 'imply' anything of the sort to Rousseau. The modern reader of the *Social Contract* might be conscious of the dangers of placing power in the hands of the people, and may regard popular sovereignty as synonymous with some form of popular tyranny. At the time when Rousseau was writing the experience of totalitarian democracy had yet to come, and therefore what Rousseau and his contemporaries understood by the phrase 'sovereignty of the people' could obviously not be what the twentieth-century student of politics understands by it. On the other hand the social and political evils which Rousseau attacked were real to the eighteenth-century mind. Inequality, privilege and despotism were a part of the experience of Rousseau and his contemporaries. It was necessary to stress equality of rights and equality under the law because these things were lacking in eighteenth-century society. The questions which Rousseau asked himself were: How can liberty and equality be guaranteed? By what means is it possible to maintain the rule of law? He perceived that so long as the power of making the law was to be vested in one individual, the people would continue to be subject to an arbitrary will. He perceived that so long as minorities could claim privileges and exemptions it would be impossible to establish a just society. In his theory of sovereignty he was groping after a new concept of society in which liberty, equality and the rule of law would be guaranteed by the equal right of every citizen to participate in making the laws. It must be remembered that in the eighteenth century the people were the still untried receptacle for power, and the eighteenth century held, on the whole, an optimistic view of human nature. Rousseau himself believed that men's innate potentialities could be developed in a just society in such a way that the people would rise to the role of responsible citizenship. He did not believe that any one man, once aware of his political rights, would deliberately and consciously act in such a way as to destroy his own liberty. These assumptions show the wide gap which separates eighteenth-centry conceptions from those based on subsequent experience.

When Rousseau wrote that the general will could not be represented and could only be expressed by the entire people, he did not intend to invest in the people all those powers which he was taking away from the despot. Rousseau, it has been pointed out, was the greatest of Montesquieu's disciples, and as such an exponent of the separation of powers.[1] The form of government which he thought the best was an elective aristocracy, in which the powers of legislation would be vested in the people and the judicial and administrative functions in the magistrates.[2] Sovereignty was indivisible and inalienable, but the work of government ought, he believed, to be delegated. Admittedly this distinction between legislation and government was easier to draw in Rousseau's day than it is in ours. The executive was expected to govern within the framework of certain fundamental laws which it could not change. This was the view expressed in the Remonstrances of the Parlements,[3] and it was the view which Rousseau also took.

Moreover, Rousseau made it clear that only in certain circumstances could his theories be applied with any degree of success. For the general will to find expression it was necessary that the society should be very small and closely knit by the bonds of custom and common interest. In such a society the occasions when the people were called upon to act in their sovereign capacity would in fact be very few. Firstly, the actual size of the state and secondly, the strength of custom would reduce the need for great activity on the part of the legislative power. Indeed Rousseau did not believe it to be either necessary or advisable that the sovereign should be perpetually in action. In the *Discours sur l'Économie Politique* he stated that

[1] A. Cobban, *Rousseau and the Modern State*, 1964, p. 49.

[2] *C.S.*, III, ch. v; Vaughan, II, 74–6.

[3] See Ch. VII below.

the sovereign should not be assembled at every unforeseen event.[1]

It is clear that the same factors which made unnecessary the continual activity of the sovereign would also limit the role of the magistrates. Ideally, Rousseau believed that habit should replace authority in the regulation of men's lives.[2] The magistrates were called upon to deal with the details of government within the framework of well-known laws. Thus there is no question, in Rousseau's small society, of the individual becoming the victim of perpetual political pressure exercised by leaders who wish to give the appearance of legality to their arbitrary actions. If we are to understand Rousseau's theory of popular sovereignty we must consider the idea in a context very different from that familiar to our own century.

Again, Rousseau never advocated that the individual should be stripped of his property and deprived of all personal ties and loyalties to stand in defenceless isolation in the face of an omnipotent state. We must distinguish between what he wrote of the large monarchical state and what he wrote of the small society in which he visualized the possible realization of his theories. He clearly argued that in great states intermediate bodies should be as many and as varied as possible, because they provided the bulwarks of tradition against the corrosive tide of despotism.[3] He did not, however, regard the great monarchical state as the political organization best designed for man's happiness. His aim was to consider the conditions in which there would be no need for those estates and corporations whose jealously guarded privileges divided French society and utterly perverted the justice and equality of the laws. In a small republic they would be superfluous because the people would be bound closely together by the strong ties of common interest, tradition and kinship, and every citizen would feel himself to be a part of the society to which he belonged.

As for the system of property in itself, the subject is one to which Rousseau made frequent reference, and there does not appear to have been any confusion in his mind on this issue.

[1] *E.P.*, Vaughan, I, 247.
[2] *C.S.*, ch. xii, Vaughan, II, 64.
[3] Ibid. III, ch. vi, Vaughan, II, 78. See also *E.P.*, Vaughan, I, 242.

He frequently attacked inequalities of wealth, but such attacks were not unusual in eighteenth-century philosophy and should not be regarded as attacks on the institution of property as such. Rousseau with characteristic intensity went so far as to say that the first man who enclosed a piece of land and said, 'This is mine', was the originator of all the subsequent ills which befell societies.[1] Even here, however, he was not attacking the institution of property. His view of property was similar to that held by Locke; he believed that property was that with which a man had mixed his labour. In a man's property, he wrote in *Émile*, there is a part of himself, and he can claim it against all the world.[2] But whereas Locke regarded it as perfectly in keeping with the natural order for a man to commute his right to property in return for a wage, Rousseau held that the concentration of property in the hands of a few destroyed men's natural independence—it caused some individuals to be dependent on the wills of others, which Rousseau regarded as contrary to nature. It is in this sense that he attacked property in the *Second Discourse*. Rousseau held that each man had a natural right to the amount of property necessary to satisfy his own essential needs, and that no one had a right to more.[3] He regarded it as the duty of the state to maintain this principle, in order that the equality and independence which men enjoyed in the natural state should he perpetuated in the civil state, and in order that society should be protected from the moral evils and political dangers attendant upon great extremes of wealth on the one hand and poverty on the other. Only in one sense could Rousseau be regarded as favouring a class-less society; that is, in so far as his ideal society was 'middle-class'.

A modern student of Rousseau, trying to judge whether or not his theories were totalitarian would probably regard as even more significant his attitude to minorities; but here also it would be misleading to judge Rousseau's thought outside the context of his own times. The idea of institutionalizing dissentient opinion by means of political parties was quite alien to the

[1] *D.I.*, Part II; Vaughan, I, 169.
[2] *Émile*, II, *Œuvres*, X, 208–9.
[3] *C.S.*, I, ch. ix; Vaughan, II, 28.

theory and practice of eighteenth-century politics. Political theorists presupposed both the possibility and the advisability of unanimity in society. The British political divisions were regarded, by continental observers, as an aberration, peculiar to these islands. Moreover, the British ruling classes themselves did not conceive of sovereignty in terms of the interplay of interests and the balancing of views all equally deserving of a hearing.[1]

Rousseau tried to eliminate the whole difficult problem of minorities from consideration in his political theory. In the first place he sought to ensure that society was based on a fundamental community of interests by the very existence of the social compact. This first convention was the guarantee of the legitimacy of all future regulations, for unless all had agreed on the prior convention by which society was established, then the law must inevitably be tyrannical in respect of some of its members.

En effet, s'il n'y avait point de convention antérieure, où serait, à moins que l'élection ne fût unanime, l'obligation pour le petit nombre de se soumettre au choix du grand? et d'où cent qui veulent un maître ont-ils le droit de voter pour dix qui n'en veulent point? La loi de la pluralité des suffrages est elle-même un établissement de convention, et suppose, au moins une fois, l'unanimité.[2]

Rousseau accepted the logical conclusions of his principles. If there came to exist within a society a group of citizens whose interests were fundamentally opposed to those of the rest, then in his view there was no longer one society. There were two societies and two general wills. This identity of interest may be regarded as idealistic, and Rousseau recognized that in practice it would be impossible to achieve except in a very small, conservative state. A large state, he believed, must inevitably be tyrannical toward some section of its people:

Les mêmes lois ne peuvent convenir à tant de provinces diverses qui ont des mœurs différentes, qui vivent sous de climats opposés, et qui ne peuvent souffrir la même forme de gouvernement.[3]

As the boundaries of the state were enlarged, so the relation

[1] Talmon, *Origins*, p. 44.
[2] *C.S.*, I, ch. v; Vaughan, II, 31–2.
[3] Ibid. I, ch. vii; Vaughan, II, 36.

between customs and laws became weaker and the coercive power of the state had to be proportionately increased. Only when the state was restricted to the limits of a group whose interests and customs were homogeneous was it possible to formulate the general will and to promulgate laws which would not violate the conscience of any minority or individual.

Assuming these conditions Rousseau held that any individual who did not will the general will could justifiably be forced nevertheless to conform to it. He drew the well-known conclusion:

Ce qui ne signifie autre chose sinon qu'on le forcera d'être libre.[1]

This was certainly dangerously epigrammatic, but even the most liberal governments insist that all the members of the state must conform to certain minimum standards of behaviour, without which the existence of society would not be possible at all. Moreover, since some ethical standards accepted by a society are higher than those which would otherwise be accepted by many individuals who are members of it, the coercive power of the state is commonly regarded as justifiably used to ensure conformity to these standards. The crucial point is reached, of course, when, in a conflict between the state and the individual, there is doubt whether the ethical standards upheld by the state are in fact higher than those maintained by the individual. This situation, however, is precisely the one which Rousseau tried to avoid. At least we can say that when Rousseau put forward his theory of the general will he was not providing a pretext by which people should be forced to conform to a system of ideas imposed upon them. The general will is not, in fact, an anticipation of the 'party line'. Rousseau, writing in the middle of the eighteenth century, could not possibly have envisaged the techniques which have been devised and utilized by the modern state to mould mass opinion. The very idea that human beings can be 'conditioned' to accept a body of beliefs and to act in a way convenient to their rulers is alien to Rousseau's thought. This idea is modern. Elements of it may be found in the works of some eighteenth-century writers, but it is diametrically opposed to Rousseau's views about the educative

[1] *C.S.*, I, ch. vii; Vaughan, II, 36.

role of society.[1] Education for Rousseau was essentially a process of self-realization.

Rousseau regarded the general will as the means whereby the individual's consciousness of justice might be given expression in the laws. His intention was not to sacrifice the individual to the collective entity, but to consider how society could best be adapted to the essential nature of man. Like his contemporaries and immediate predecessors, Rousseau began his search for social justice by considering human beings outside society. He considered, that is, the essential nature of man before he considered the kind of society in which men can live happily. Like Pufendorf, Rousseau held that all men had implanted in them by nature 'un principe intérieur pour se gouverner eux-mêmes.'[2] Thus they were in this respect independent of one another, each following his own inner voice. It was in this sense that he regarded men as equal, for it was against nature for one man to be subordinated to the will of another. Rousseau sought to ensure that in society the right of the individual to control his own destiny would be preserved. He believed that the only way to achieve this was for all men to be equal under the laws which all had equally participated in making. Thus the Rousseauist theory of the general will is based on the principle that each man has a right to control his own life.

It was, however, not enough in Rousseau's view that all should participate in making the laws. For the general will to be expressed it was necessary that the decisions which the people reached should be just. This does not mean that they should be forced to accept and to will according to an external standard incompatible with the individual conscience. On the contrary, it was only when the individual conscience became the criterion of judgement that Rousseau believed the general

[1] The most extreme eighteenth-century statement of the power of education was put forward by Helvétius. See *De l'Homme*, II, sect. x, ch. i, 'L'éducation peut tout'. See also his attack on the *Émile* in sect. v, chs. i–ix. Rousseau also attacked the theories of Helvétius: see *Corr. Gén.*, 5 October 1758, IV, let. 546. The disagreement between Rousseau and Helvétius is discussed by Grossman, *The Philosophy of Helvétius*, 1926, ch. xi. See also Dutens, *Lettre à M. D. . . . B. . . . sur la réfutation du Livre de l'Esprit d'Helvétius par J. J. Rousseau*, 1779. The arguments ascribed to Rousseau in this book were printed, according to Dutens, from MS. notes made by Rousseau in the margin of Dutens' copy of *De l'Esprit*.

[2] Pufendorf, *Droit de la nature et des gens*. See I, ch. vi, p. 91.

will could be expressed. Indeed, he specifically stated that for the general will to be expressed each individual should 'think only his own thoughts'.[1] He expressed this idea even more clearly in the *Discours sur l'Économie Politique* where he asserted that for the general will to be expressed it was necessary for each citizen to 'act according to the rules of his own judgement and not to behave inconsistently with himself'.[2]

Rousseau did not detect any menace to individual liberty in the assumption that to every political issue that arose there was only one answer conformable with justice, and that the whole people could be expected to accept that answer. He held the view that was common to his age, that men were possessed of a single, unitary will. The conflicts which arose in men's minds were not, he believed, natural to them. They were the products of corrupt conventions which exacted conformity to social standards incompatible with the individual sense of justice. It was on this sense of justice that the general will was based. Where men's minds had not been corrupted by evil institutions there was no obstacle, in Rousseau's view, to the expression of the general will, and no reason why the citizens should not reach agreement on all matters of fundamental importance.

This view may be considered as unduly optimistic, but at least it is not the case that Rousseau thought in terms of adapting men to society. On the contrary, his aim was to preserve and to give a new moral context to man's natural liberty. Two inseparable conditions were necessary for legislation: every individual must have participated in making the laws, and the laws themselves had to be the expression of the individual sense of justice.

How was it possible to ensure that in the course of his transposition from the natural to the social state, man's will was not corrupted? This is a crucial point in Rousseau's political thought. It was in the course of this change that the innate potentialities of the individual were realized. In the *Second Discourse* he argued that it was only as a result of living together in communities that men began to appreciate the idea of

[1] *C.S.* II, ch. iii; Vaughan, II, 43.

[2] *E.P.*, Vaughan, I, 245. This passage also appears in the first draft of the *C.S.* I, ch. vii; Vaughan I, 245.

justice, and to realize that new standards of behaviour were demanded of them which were not necessary so long as they were solitary creatures. Unfortunately, by the time this realization came, it was often too late. Some individuals had already seen how they could take advantage of the new conditions to further their own selfish ends. Thus when the state took form it was based on injustice and perpetuated the inequality and privilege which had already arisen.

In the *Social Contract* Rousseau described how a society, at the very outset of its existence, could establish conventions by which the process of corruption described in the *Second Discourse* could be avoided. It was in this context that he visualized the work of the great legislator, a man who could see further than his fellow citizens and who would establish just conventions at the very foundations of society. Thus the individual's innate potentialities would be developed in relation to a virtuous concept of citizenship. Instead of being corrupted by contact with his fellow men he would realize, in society, his full moral stature. It is therefore in relation to this great crossroads in the history of mankind, the assumption of social responsibility, that Rousseau's description of the legislator should be considered.

Essentially, Rousseau was a conservative, imbued with classical philosophy, free from the idea of progress and looking to the past rather than to the future. He regarded the legislator as the great man who achieved his superhuman task in the dawn of history. Thereafter the longevity of a society depended on the degree to which its people remained faithful to their ancient traditions of virtue. Any departure from custom was a falling away from the primitive standards of virtue and a step downward in the inevitable process of decay and disruption to which all societies were subject.[1] Thus, unlike nineteenth- and twentieth-century philosophers, Rousseau looked back to his superman, not forward. His concept of the legislator may reasonably be supposed to have originated in his study of ancient history, and particularly of Plutarch, rather than in any intuitive glimpse of the modern dictator. The great legislators he quoted were Lycurgus, Solon and Moses. He did not

[1] *C.S.* III, chs. x, xi; Vaughan, II, 88–92.

envisage the great leader as Professor Toynbee describes him, as the man who 'breaks the crust of custom' and thus releases forces which carry society a stage further in the process of its development.[1] On the contrary, Rousseau regarded the task of the great man as setting society firmly in the mould of custom. He quoted Montesquieu: 'At the birth of societies rulers of republics establish institutions and afterwards the institutions mould the rulers.'[2]

Rousseau admittedly considered the possibility of an old state being regenerated by a violent revolution, but he thought that the cases when this happened were extremely rare and the intention dangerous. It was precisely at such times that usurpers were likely to establish themselves, so that the people, far from gaining their liberty, bound themselves more tightly than before.

> Les usurpateurs amènent ou choisissent toujours ces temps de troubles pour faire passer, à la faveur de l'effroi public, des lois destructives que le peuple n'adopterait jamais de sang-froid. Le choix du moment de l'institution est un des caractères les plus sûrs par lesquels on peut distinguer l'œuvre du Législateur d'avec celle du tyran.[3]

In order to understand Rousseau's intentions it is necessary to consider his theory of the general will within the self-contained logic of his political theory, and to place this against the background of his own century. It must be recognized that the ideal principles of the *Social Contract* were developed in relation to an ideal society. Rousseau did not believe that the general will could find expression except in a very small state in which the citizens were closely bound by common interests and traditions, and by a high regard for the virtuous customs of their ancestors. To neglect what Rousseau wrote about small states and then to criticize his theories in relation to the modern Leviathan must inevitably lead to distortion. Rousseau obviously knew nothing of modern forms of dictatorship, but he did attack those forms of dictatorship with which he was familiar. Whereas the Physiocrats favoured 'legal' or 'enlightened'

[1] Toynbee, *Study of History*, ed. Somervell, 1949, I, 49.
[2] *C.S.* II, ch. vii; Vaughan, II, 51.
[3] Ibid. II, ch. x; Vaughan, II, 60.

despotism, Rousseau, on the contrary, stated that legal despotism was a contradiction in terms, and held that the individual was the best judge of his own interests.[1]

Rousseau's aim was to discuss the conditions in which men could preserve their natural liberty, equality and independence. His success or failure must be judged in relation to the kind of society which he believed would provide those conditions, and not in relation to some other society which he could not have foreseen and which he certainly would have condemned if he had. It is indeed possible to argue that Rousseau's theory contained some elements which would be unacceptable to later liberal thought. For example, the state which he visualized was essentially static. It was assumed that once the contract had been established no further social development was desirable. The state would have to be limited in members to those whose economic interests were easily reconciled, and would have to exclude economic interests which were divergent. Any discussion of differences arising in the same society with a view to compromise would appear to be ruled out by Rousseau's theory. The demand that the individual should think only his own thoughts seems to suggest that discussion was not regarded as a means whereby unanimity could properly be reached. The very assumption that for any society there was only one course of action which could be regarded as just, and that every individual in that society must accept that course as just, owning himself mistaken if he had originally thought otherwise, makes Rousseau's theory of the general will seem oppressive.

However, such considerations only throw into higher relief the great divergences between Rousseau's political thought and the character of modern totalitarian democracy. The repressive qualities of Rousseau's small state are more akin to those of Calvinist Geneva or Plato's ideal state, than to the great totalitarian state of the twentieth century. The citizen who shuts himself up to think his own thoughts whenever a decision must be made in the state has more affinities with the Puritan, closeted alone with his Bible, than with the party member struggling to bring his thoughts into line with an externally imposed philosophy.

[1] *Lettre à M. le Marquis de Mirabeau,* 26 July 1764, Vaughan, II, 161.

Thus we must guard against the tendency to see the *Social Contract* as the first step in a process of revolution by which, over the past two hundred years, traditional governments have been overthrown and the sovereignty of the people established; and equally against seeing the French Revolution as the first practical expression of the process which Rousseau initiated. But we must now turn to the specific problem of the relation between the thought of Rousseau and the practice of the Revolution.

PART II

The Revolutionary Rousseau

CHAPTER IV

The Study of Rousseau's Political Theory, 1762–1788

In attempting to assess the influence of the theories contained in the *Social Contract* it is necessary to begin by asking, first, what evidence exists that the *Social Contract* was read, and secondly, what, if anything, its readers said and wrote about it. Although this study is mainly concerned with the period 1789–91, it will be impossible to understand the attitudes of mind of the revolutionary generation towards Rousseau's political theory unless account is also taken of views held before 1789. Was the *Social Contract* read by a growing number of people after its first publication in 1762, so that it may be regarded as having provided a common inspiration to the generation which made the Revolution? Alternatively, was there a period immediately before the Revolution, when discontent with the Ancien Régime brought about a new or a revived interest in the *Social Contract*? Could it be argued that the events of 1789 were seen through the eyes of earnest students of the *Social Contract*, or that those who shaped the events of 1789–91 looked to Rousseau's works for their political inspiration?

A study of Rousseauist and eighteenth-century bibliographies indicates that by comparison with the works of other writers, and by comparison with other works by Rousseau, the *Social Contract* was not in great demand between 1762 and 1790.[1] 'Si l'on compare avec le nombre des éditions et les commentaires

[1] J. Senélier, *Bibliographie générale des œuvres de J. J. Rousseau*, 1948. See also Quérard, *La France littéraire*, 1827–39, VII; Monglond, *La France révolutionnaire et impériale*, 1930–35, I–III; Dufour and Plan, *Recherches bibliographiques sur J. J. Rousseau*, 1925. On the editions of the *Nouvelle Héloise*, see Mornet, *Les Éditions de la Nouvelle Héloise*, in *Annales* V (1909).

de la Henriade . . . de Candide, de l'Histoire des Deux Indes de Raynal, etc.', wrote Mornet, 'on peut dire que le Contrat Social a passé à peu près inaperçu'.[1] In his study of the catalogues of five hundred libraries in the vicinity of Paris for the years 1750–80, Mornet discovered that out of thirty-six works, the importance of which he tried to assess, the *Social Contract* came last on his list, only one copy having been discovered.[2] 'De ce livre redoutable', he wrote, 'c'est à peine si l'on parle avant 1789. . . . Il faut dépouiller cinq cent catalogues de Bibliothèques de XVIIIe siècle, où l'on trouve cent quatre-vingt-cinq exemplaires de la Nouvelle Héloise, pour rencontrer un exemplaire de ce livre.'[3]

The first edition of the *Social Contract* was published in 1762, by Rey of Amsterdam. There were no further editions until 1772, when one edition was published, again by Rey. After 1772, no edition appeared until 1790. Thus no edition was published in the years immediately preceding the Revolution, nor in the first year of the Revolution. In 1790, two editions were published, one at Paris and one at Geneva. In 1791, four editions appeared, two of which were published in Paris, one at Geneva and one at Strasbourg.

The first edition of the *Social Contract* was not widely distributed in France. In his *Confessions* Rousseau described how Rey applied to the censor's office for permission to bring his consignments of the *Social Contract* into France by way of Rouen, where he sent them by sea. He obtained no reply, and the parcels remained there for several months. Rousseau recounts that an attempt was made to confiscate them, but as a result of Rey's protests they were sent back to him.[4] This story is con-

[1] D. Mornet, *Les Origines intellectuelles*, p. 96.

[2] D. Mornet, 'Les enseignements des bibliothèques privées, 1750–1780', *Revue de l'histoire littéraire de la France*, XVII (1910), pp. 449–95. Mornet pointed out in this study that the statistics he produced were unfavourable to the works of Rousseau since his survey began in 1750. Thus books which had been in publication prior to that date would be represented in preponderant numbers. The *Social Contract*, which was not published until 1762, could not in any case have been purchased for the first twelve years of the period under consideration. Again, as Mornet observed, the owners of the libraries, the catalogues of which he studied, were members of the *noblesse* and the *haute bourgeoisie*.

[3] D. Mornet, 'L'influence de J. J. Rousseau au XVIIIe siècle', *Annales*, VIII (1912), p. 44.

[4] *Conf.* XI, *Œuvres*, XXV, 376–7.

firmed in Rey's correspondence with Rousseau. Not only were the books consigned to Paris returned to him, but the Genevan booksellers also refused to take copies.[1] Rey was left with an edition of five thousand copies on his hands, which he disposed of in England, Germany and elsewhere.[2] Rousseau stated that a few people in France who wanted to read the book had to get it from Amsterdam.[3]

In these circumstances it is not surprising that the *Social Contract* excited much less controversy than Rousseau's other works. The number of books devoted to the *Social Contract*, both in the years immediately after its publication, and in the years which followed, is negligible by comparison with the vast amount of literature inspired by the *Nouvelle Héloise* and *Émile*. Derathé discovered four refutations of the *Social Contract* written between 1762 and 1766, and of these four, only two were actually published at the time. These were: *L'Anti-Contrat Social* by Ph. de Beauclair, which appeared in 1764 and the *Lettre d'un Anonyme*, by Élie Luzac, published in 1766.[4] Some other refutations of the *Social Contract* were published, but the authors of these works did not concern themselves with Rousseau's political principles. They limited their arguments to rejecting Rousseau's theories on the civil religion, and his views on Christianity.[5] 'La littérature polémique immédiate', wrote Jean Fabre, 'si abondante pour les Discours, et l'Émile, n'encombra guère les historiens du Contrat Social.'[6]

Such interest as the official condemnation of the *Social Contract* in Paris and Geneva raised appears to have waned quickly. It is significant that Berthier's *Observations sur le Contrat Social de J. J. Rousseau* was not published until 1789.[7] The author set out

[1] *Corr. Gén.* VII, 221, 255, 259.

[2] R. B. Mowat, *Jean-Jacques Rousseau*, 1938, p. 209.

[3] *Conf.* XI, *Oeuvres*, XXV, 377.

[4] R. Derathé, 'Les réfutations du Contrat Social au dix-huitième siècle', *Annales*, XXXII (1950).

[5] See, for example, Roustan, *Offrande aux autels de la patrie, contenant la défense du Christianisme, ou réfutations du Contrat Social*, etc., 1764; l'abbé d'Arnavon, *Discours apologétique de la Religion Chrétienne au sujet de plusieurs assertions du Contrat Social*, etc., 1773; Anon., *Le Préservatif*, 1765.

[6] J. Fabre, 'Pierre Naville: Examen du Contrat Social de J. J. Rousseau, etc., publié d'après le manuscrit autographe,' *Annales*, XXII (1933), p. 9.

[7] C. F. Berthier, *Observations sur le Contrat Social de J. J. Rousseau*, 1789.

to make a detailed analysis of Rousseau's text in order to refute his entire political system, but after the official condemnation of the *Social Contract* he did not regard his work as of sufficient importance either to publish or even to complete it. The *Examen du Contrat Social* of Pierre Naville, written between 1762 and 1766 was not published until 1933, when it was edited by Jean Fabre.[1] In the extracts from journals made by P.-P. Plan, there is a total of no less than twenty-seven separate references to Rousseau's name during the year 1762, but of these only four refer to the *Social Contract*, the majority relating to the publication of *Émile*. Indeed, during the whole period 1762–89, there are only eight references to the *Social Contract* out of a total of two hundred and forty-eight references to Rousseau's life and works. Of these, four appear for the year 1762, as stated above, and the others for the years 1763, 1764, 1765 and 1778 respectively.[2]

Between 1766 and 1789 only one writer undertook any notable discussion of Rousseau's political principles. This was the abbé J. C. F. Legros, who published his analysis of Rousseau's works in 1785.[3] This writer was concerned with the wider philosophical implications of Rousseau's theories as a whole, rather than with the immediate implications of his political theories, and attempted to show the unity of Rousseau's thought as it developed, mainly in relation to the two *Discours* and to *Émile*. While he concluded that Rousseau was a revolutionary who wanted to change man and society, he apparently regarded his theories as too abstract to permit of any treatment other than a tolerant and philosophical detachment, and as having no direct political significance in relation to existing societies.

It is difficult to make any assessment of the attitude of French readers towards the *Social Contract* between 1762 and 1789. One opinion, however, appears to have been fairly general; the *Social Contract* was regarded as an abstract work which was extremely difficult to understand. A correspondent of the publisher Rey wrote to him in 1762:

[1] Fabre, *Annales*, XXII.

[2] P.-P. Plan, *J. J. Rousseau raconté par les gazettes de son temps*, 1912.

[3] J. C. F. Legros, *Analyse des ouvrages de J. J. Rousseau de Genève, et de M. Court de Gébelin, par un Solitaire*, 1785.

J'ai lu son Contrat Social avec avidité, mais je vous avoue avec humilité cependant que je trouve cet ouvrage si décousu et si peu lumineux pour moi en certain endroits que je n'ose pas me prononcer sur son mérite.[1]

The abstract character of Rousseau's political treatise was also noted in 1762 in the *Mémoires Secrètes de Bachaumont*, where it is recorded that:

On parle beaucoup du livre de Rousseau qui doit servir de cinquième volume de son Traité de l'Éducation; c'est son Contrat Social. On pretend qu'il y en a des exemplaires à Paris, mais en très petit nombre. On le dit extrêmement abstrait.[2]

Later in the same year the writer deplored the dangerous character of the work but comforted himself and his readers by reflecting that fortunately very few people would understand it:

Heureusement que l'auteur s'est enveloppé dans une obscurité scientifique, qui le rend impénétrable au commun des lecteurs.[3]

The anonymous author of the *Dictionnaire Social et Patriotique*, published in 1770, also remarked upon the abstract quality of the *Social Contract*. This, however, he regarded as more apparent than real, and due to the fact that Rousseau had affected new phraseology to express ideas which were already stale.[4] Even Mme. Roland, who in 1777 remonstrated indignantly with Sophie Cannet because the latter refused to admire Rousseau's works, nevertheless admitted in a later letter to Henriette Cannet that she could not understand the *Social Contract* herself.

Je voudrais bien revoir encore toutes les œuvres de ce bon maître [she wrote], au défaut des autres je lis et relis ses discours, et son Contrat Social, que je ne me flatte pas d'entendre d'un bout à l'autre.[5]

Writing after the Revolution, Sénac de Meilhan confirmed these comments by observing: 'Le Contrat Social, profond et abstrait, était peu lu et entendu de bien peu de gens'.[6]

[1] *Corr. Gén.*, 9 September 1762, VIII, 118.
[2] Plan, *J. J. Rousseau*, etc., pp. 20–1.
[3] Ibid. p. 27.
[4] Anon., *Dictionnaire social et patriotique* etc., 1770. See p. 109, *Démocratie*.
[5] *Lettres de Mme Roland aux Demoiselles Cannet*, etc., 1867, II, 186–7, 206.
[6] Mornet, *Les Origines intellectuelles* etc., p. 96.

It would seem therefore that there is very little evidence to support the argument that Rousseau's *Social Contract* was widely read at any time between 1762 and 1789. Perhaps, however, it could be argued that in order to assess Rousseau's political influence one should not seek to establish the extent to which the *Social Contract* was read but rather to discover who read it. That is to say, that while only a few people read the *Social Contract* prior to 1789, nevertheless they may have included among their numbers some of those who played an active or even a leading part in the events of 1789.

This argument, however, is not supported by the evidence which the memoirs of the revolutionary generation supply. References to Rousseau's name and to his works are fairly frequent in revolutionary journals and memoirs, but references to the *Social Contract* are rare. This applies, moreover, even to those who in view of their expressed interest in Rousseau's life and works have been regarded as his particular disciples. Meynier, for example, singled out La Revellière-Lépeaux as an outstanding example of the influence exercised by Rousseau's theories upon the deputies of 1789–91.[1] Yet although La Revellière-Lépeaux recorded that he held regular Sunday meetings during the period of the National Assembly and the Convention in the same house in which his family had frequently received Rousseau, he made no reference to the *Social Contract*. Moreover, although a short essay on the subject of federalism is included in his memoirs, he gave no indication that he was aware of Rousseau's views on this subject.[2] Similarly, Aulard wrote of Louvet that he was a whole-hearted disciple of Rousseau, basing his religion on the *Profession de foi*, and ascribing to 'Lodoiska' all the characteristics of 'Julie'.[3] While however Louvet referred to Rousseau as 'his master', his journal contains no references to the *Social Contract*.[4]

The same is true of other revolutionary writers. Barère was the author of an *éloge* to Rousseau published in 1788, and in

[1] A. Meynier, *Un représentant de la bourgeoisie angevine*, 1905. See also *J. J. Rousseau, révolutionnaire*, 1911.

[2] *Mémoires de la Revellière-Lépeaux*, ed. R. David, 1895, I.

[3] F. A. Aulard, *Orateurs de la Révolution*, 1905, II, 3. 9. See also *Mémoires de Louvet de Couvrai*, ed. Aulard, 1889, Introduction.

[4] See *Mémoires de Louvet de Couvrai.*

November 1790 was chosen to second the motion proposing the erection of a statue to Rousseau and the payment of a pension to his widow. Yet Barère's *Mémoires* contain no references to the *Social Contract.*[1] No reference was made by the abbé Grégoire to the *Social Contract* in his *Mémoires*, although he also was the author of an *éloge* to Rousseau.[2] Brissot recorded that the reading of *Émile* was a turning point in his life; the *Profession de foi*, he wrote was 'le premier ouvrage qui me fît tomber le bandeau des yeux'. Whenever he was troubled by doubts it was, he wrote, to the wisdom of the Savoyard Vicar that he turned. Yet his enthusiasm for *Émile* did not apparently lead him to study the *Social Contract*, for his *Mémoires* contain no reference to this work.[3] In 1789 this disciple of Rousseau put forward a plan for the limitation of the powers of the representative assembly and for the sanctioning of all legislation by primary assemblies, yet he made no reference to the views which Rousseau expressed on these subjects in the *Social Contract.* It was in 1791 that Brissot referred to Rousseau's views on representation, which seems to suggest that he read the *Social Contract* only after 1789.[4]

Mme. Roland recorded in her *Vie Privée* the impression made upon her when, at the age of twenty-one, she first read the *Nouvelle Héloise*; her correspondence contains frequent references to Rousseau's works and to his views on a number of subjects. Yet while, unlike many of her contemporaries it appears, she read the *Social Contract*, as has been indicated above she admitted that she could not understand it.[5] Sieyès, who is regarded by Professor Talmon has having tried to put Rousseau's theories into practice, did not refer to the *Social Contract* in any published work.[6] D'Escherny, who was an admirer of Rousseau's works, and a personal friend of Rousseau himself until the latter's death, does not appear to have been greatly impressed or influenced by the *Social Contract.* In 1790

[1] B. Barère, *Mémoires*, ed. Carnot, 1842.

[2] H. B. Grégoire, *Mémoires*, ed. Carnot, 1837.

[3] J. P. Brissot, *Mémoires*, 1754–93, ed. Perroud, 1910.

[4] Compare *Plan de conduite pour les députés du peuple aux États Généraux de 1789* and *Discours sur les conventions prononcé . . . le 8 Août, 1791.*

[5] *Vie Privée*, *Œuvres*, Ann. VIII, 1, 154, 207.

[6] For Sieyès' views on Rousseau see Ch. VIII.

he doubled the prize of 300 francs offered by the Académie to the writer of the best *éloge* on Rousseau's life and works, and he anonymously entered for this prize himself. Yet neither in the *Éloge* which he submitted, nor in his *Mémoires* is there any discussion of Rousseau's political views. In the *Éloge* d'Escherny considered the continuity and significance of the ideas which Rousseau developed in his first and second *Discours*. In his *Mémoires*, d'Escherny's references to Rousseau were confined to personal reminiscences. It was only in the *Correspondance d'un habitant de Paris*, published in 1791, that he discussed the theories of the *Social Contract*, but this was in order to show that Rousseau's political theories had exercised no influence on the Revolution.[1]

Thus the study of memoirs confirms the evidence of the bibliographies, and leads to the conclusion that the *Social Contract* did not play an important part in shaping the views of those who participated in the events of 1789. It was only after 1789 that interest in the *Social Contract* began to develop.

[1] D'Escherny's account of his relations with Rousseau is given in *Mélanges de Littérature*, 1811. This contains the *Éloge de J. J. Rousseau*, written during 1789–90, and an essay, *Des Erreurs de J. J. Rousseau en politique*, written after the Revolution. D'Escherny gave his views on the influence of Rousseau's political theory during the first three years of the Revolution in his *Correspondance d'un habitant de Paris avec ses amis de Suisse et d'Angleterre*, 1791. See Introduction, 'De l'influence de J. J. Rousseau sur la Révolution de France'. An account of d'Escherny's relations with Rousseau is also given by Buffenoir, *Le Prestige de J. J. Rousseau*, 1909.

CHAPTER V

The Appeal to Rousseau's Authority, and Rousseauist Literature, 1788–1791

FROM the study of books, pamphlets, journals and the reports of the debates in the National Assembly and in the various clubs it is possible to draw conclusions about the ways in which the revolutionaries thought about Rousseau and the extent to which they used his name.

It is necessary, in the first place, to distinguish between interest in Rousseau's political theory and that passionate interest in all those other aspects of his life and work which had been more or less continuous since the 1760's. Mornet considered that the literary and personal cult of Rousseau began in the last years of his life and continued to grow in numbers and emotional intensity after his death, reaching its height about ten years before the Revolution.[1] In 1782 interest in Rousseau's life received a new stimulus from the publication of the first part of the *Confessions*. Even after 1789, however, when Rousseau's name came to be increasingly associated with the Revolution, his political theory still continued to excite less interest than other aspects of his life and works. He was presented in literature and drama as a great writer, thinker, moralist and educationist; his work as a botanist and a musician was described and praised, his personal life defended. It was still generally agreed, even after 1789, that his most important works were the *Nouvelle Héloise* and the *Émile*.

Thus there already existed, before the Revolution, a Rousseauist cult. This was carried on after the Revolution, but we must not confuse the adulation of his name or interest in his

[1] See D. Mornet, *Rousseau, l'Homme et l'œuvre*, 1950, p. 175 ff.

works with knowledge of his political theory. For example, in 1789, two works on Rousseau were published by the comte de Barruel-Beauvert and by Mme. de Staël respectively. The former mentioned the *Social Contract* among Rousseau's works; he made no reference to its contents or to Rousseau's political thought.[1] Mme. de Staël similarly regarded Rousseau's political thought as his least important achievement. She asserted that the *Nouvelle Héloise* was the most widely read, and *Émile* the greatest of his works. She found the *Social Contract* impractical and abstract.[2]

During 1788–91 numerous *éloges* were addressed to Rousseau's memory. The remarkable feature of these is that their authors paid little or no attention to his political theory at a time when his name was being increasingly associated, in public and official demonstrations, with the successful progress of the Revolution. The writers were interested primarily in the first and second *Discours*, in *Émile* and the *Nouvelle Héloise*. Only one of the *éloges* published between these dates contains any considerable account of Rousseau's political theory. The author of this work, which was published in 1791, was the advocate Thiery, who devoted several pages to the *Social Contract*. Thiery was, however, careful to avoid any specific reference to those theories which ran counter to the popular concept of Rousseau as a revolutionary prophet. He was presented as arguing, as countless revolutionary pamphleteers had done, that in small states the ideal of direct popular sovereignty could be realized, but that in large states it is necessary and advisable to elect representatives and to delegate to them the sovereign power of legislation.[3] Thiery was, however, exceptional; Barère[4] and Bilhon,[5] writing in 1788, d'Escherny,[6] writing in 1789, Meude-Monpas,[7] the abbé Grégoire,[8] and Delorthe,[9] writing in 1790,

[1] A. J. de Barruel-Beauvert, *Vie de J. J. Rousseau*, 1789.

[2] A. L. G. de Staël, *Lettres sur les ouvrages et le caractère de J. J. Rousseau*, 1789, p. 54.

[3] L. V. Thiery, *Éloge de J. J. Rousseau*, 1791.

[4] B. Barère, *Éloge de J. J. Rousseau*, 1788.

[5] J. F. Bilhon, *Éloge de J. J. Rousseau*, 1788.

[6] F. L. d'Escherny, *Éloge de J. J. Rousseau*, 1790. See p. 50, n. 1 above.

[7] J. J. O. Meude-Monpas, *Éloge de J. J. Rousseau*, etc., 1790.

[8] H. B. Grégoire, *Éloge de J. J. Rousseau*, 1790.

[9] G. A. Delorthe, *Éloge de J. J. Rousseau*, 1790.

were interested in the *Émile*, the *Nouvelle Héloise* and the two *Discours*. The abbé Grégoire also discussed the *Rêveries d'un promeneur solitaire*; d'Escherney did not mention the *Social Contract* at all; the others made only passing reference to it. These *éloges* are mentioned specifically because it might be expected that their authors would have claimed for Rousseau the glory of having inspired the events of 1789. This they did not do. There is, besides, a considerable Rousseauist literature published between 1788 and 1791 which bears no relation to Rousseau's political thought and which it would be irrelevant to consider here. We must conclude that revolutionary interest in Rousseau is not coincidental with the study of his political thought.

The Pamphlets, 1788–1789

It seems fairly certain that there was not, in 1788, a revolutionary vanguard, waiting with pens poised to expound the principles of Rousseau, or ready to rush into action to frame a new France on the lines of the *Social Contract*. That the revolutionaries should be largely ignorant of Rousseau's political thought might reasonably be expected after what has already been said in the previous chapter, and this expectation is confirmed by a study of the pamphlet literature of 1788–89. I have found only one pamphleteer referring specifically to Rousseau's political theory in 1788, and he was a conservative, who pointed out that according to Rousseau the powers of the deputies elected to the Estates General ought to be severely limited. Representatives, he argued, could only act as 'intermédiaires' between King and people, and in his opinion the Parlements were already fulfilling this function admirably.[1]

The decision of the government to convene the Estates General and the invitation to the public to submit its views on the role which the Estates should fulfil, resulted in the publication of a very large number of pamphlets. But the authors of these did not appeal to the authority of any particular philosopher. The predominant pattern of these pamphlets was an

[1] Anon., *Le disciple de Montesquieu*, 1788.

examination of the traditions and precedents of past Estates. To arguments on these lines some writers added general statements about the original historic sovereignty of the people and described how, under the first three dynasties the entire adult male population had assembled annually on the Champ de Mars to participate in legislation. This principle had already become a commonplace in political controversy as a result of having been stated repeatedly by the Parlements.

Among the pamphlets dated 1789 I have discovered only seven in which reference to Rousseau's name was made. These are listed in the bibliography and are dealt with later on. It is sufficient to note, at this stage, that in one the reference to Rousseau appears in the title only, the rest of the work having no apparent connection with Rousseau or his political thought; in the next four, Rousseau's theories are rejected; in the sixth Rousseau's name is used to support the somewhat individual theories of the abbé Fauchet; and the seventh is entirely composed of extracts from the *Social Contract* chosen with a view to confirming popular opinion, but nowhere suggesting that Rousseau's theory differed from the current revolutionary attitude.[1]

THE RELATION BETWEEN ROUSSEAU'S THEORY AND THE EVENTS OF 1789–1791

Next, it is impossible to accept the views of those writers who attribute to Rousseau's influence certain aspects of revolutionary theory, or who argue that some practical measures undertaken or advocated by the revolutionaries originated in the study of his work. It is true that Rousseau's name was used in association with the broad principles of the Revolution, particularly with the ideas of liberty, equality and the sovereignty of the people, and with the idea of 'regeneration'. But when one tries to discover some more definite and specific connection between the actions of the revolutionaries and the text of the *Social Contract*, the search is unrewarding. For example, when

[1] For an analysis of the arguments used by the pamphleteers of 1788–89 see M. B. Garrett, *The Estates General of 1789*, 1935. The relations between the pamphlets of 1788–9 and the Remonstrances of the Parlements is discussed in Ch. VII below.

the National Assembly debated subjects which Rousseau had dealt with in the *Social Contract* it might be expected that some admirer of Rousseau would be able to quote from the master in support of his argument. In fact, this seems rarely to have happened. Rousseau discussed the right to emigrate and whether the power to make war and to conclude peace belonged properly to the executive or legislative. Both these subjects were debated in the Assembly, but no reference was made to Rousseau. In the course of a debate in the Jacobin Club Billaud-Varenne[1] referred to the *Social Contract* on the rights of émigrés, but another speaker asserted flatly that there was no reason why anyone should imagine that Rousseau's words carried more weight than those of any other political thinker.[2] Rousseau's name was often associated in revolutionary pamphlets with the idea of liberty and natural rights, but there appears to have been no appeal to his authority on 4 August 1789, the so-called 'night of dupes' when members of the noblesse came forward voluntarily in the assembly to renounce their titles and privileges, and when, in the fervour of revolutionary enthusiasm, feudalism was declared to be abolished throughout France. There are no recorded references to Rousseau in the *Journal des débats et des décrets* during the discussions on the Declaration of Rights, nor indeed during any session between 17 June and 1 September 1789.

Nevertheless, because Rousseau's name has been associated by historians with specific revolutionary developments, it is pertinent to discuss some of these here and to consider briefly what evidence exists to justify this association.

(i) *Direct democracy*

Mathiez, writing of the Paris Clubs, stated that 'Leur idéal emprunté de J. J. Rousseau, est le gouvernement direct'.[3]

In view of this statement, I have made a particular study of the speeches and debates reported in the *Journal des Jacobins* and also of the pamphlets relating to the Jacobins and to other Paris clubs. One general conclusion emerges: the attitude of

[1] J. N. Billaud-Varenne, *Discours sur les émigrations*, 16 Oct. 1791, p. 13.

[2] *Journal des Débats de la Société des Amis de la Constitution*, Oct. 1791, no. 79. See the report of M. Machenauer.

[3] A. Mathiez, *La Révolution française*, 1922, I, 164.

individual Jacobins toward the powers which representatives should exercise depended not upon ideological considerations but simply on their judgement as to whether or not those powers were being used correctly. Thus Robespierre, who has been regarded as a disciple of Rousseau and an early protagonist of the idea of popular participation in government, was in 1789 stating clearly and unmistakably the view that the sovereign rights of legislation belonged solely to the representatives of the people. It was only after the election of a new representative assembly, under the constitution of 1791, an assembly of which Robespierre was not a member and which in his view appeared incapable of dealing effectively with the enemies of the Revolution, that he began to question the rights of deputies.

References to Rousseau's name during the course of debates in the Jacobin Club seem to have been rare. On two occasions his name was brought in during discussions on the powers of representatives, but in neither case did the speaker appeal to his authority. On the contrary, both criticized his condemnation of representation.[1] On the other hand, both Brissot[2] and Pétion de Villeneuve[3] proposed that all legislation should be submitted to primary assemblies, but neither appealed to Rousseau's authority in support of this view. In May 1791 a federation was formed between the Cordeliers and other Paris Clubs, the central committee of which was presided over by François Robert, a republican journalist. Robert advocated the greater participation of the people in legislation, and the limitation of the power of the deputies. Yet Robert was one of Rousseau's severest critics, condemning him as an enemy of liberty because of his refusal to accept the possibility of representation.[4] Similarly the abbé Fauchet, though an admirer of Rousseau and an advocate of the limitation of the powers of deputies, was critical of Rousseau for having rejected representation altogether.[5]

[1] See F. Robert, *Le républicanisme adapté à la France*, 1790, and Brissot, *Discours sur les conventions*, 1791.

[2] J. Brissot, *Plan de conduite*, etc., 1789.

[3] J. Pétion, *Opinion sur l'appel au peuple*, 1789.

[4] Robert, *Le républicanisme* etc,

[5] Fauchet's views on representation and his discourses on the *Social Contract* are discussed more fully in Chs. VI and VIII.

(ii) *Republicanism*

Aulard asserted that Rousseau's name began to be associated with republicanism from July 1791 onward as a result of an address which Condorcet delivered to the *Cercle Social*. He wrote:

> Avant que Condorcet parlât, l'autorité de Jean-Jacques se dressait contre les républicains français. Maintenant on pourra dire républicain sans crainte d'hérésie. Le parti républicain se sent anobli, légitimé par cette intervention éclatante de l'héritier des philosophes.[1]

This is perhaps to attribute to the revolutionaries a greater respect for Rousseau's intentions, and punctiliousness in interpreting them, than is justified by the opportunist way in which his name was used. I have found no evidence of any consistent appeal to Rousseau's authority in favour of republicanism and no evidence that Condorcet's address affected opinion as Aulard suggests. In May 1791, two months before Condorcet spoke, the journal *Révolutions de Paris* published an article in which Rousseau's authority was used to support republicanism,[2] but in July 1791, Réal, speaking in the Jacobin Club, used Rousseau's authority to reject it.[3] Three pamphleteers, writing during 1790–91, acknowledged that in advocating a republican government they were proposing a form of government which Rousseau had rejected as impractical for a country as large as France.[4]

As far as the *Cercle Social* is concerned, the swing toward republicanism was accompanied by a lessening of interest in Rousseau. This was not due to ideological convictions but to the departure of Fauchet, a keen Rousseauist, to take up his duties as Constitutional Bishop of Calvados in June, 1791. During July the *Bouche de Fer*, the journal of the *Cercle Social*, came out strongly in favour of a republic, but from the end of June, references to Rousseau, hitherto a remarkable feature of

[1] Aulard, *L'Histoire politique de la Révolution française, 1789–1804*, 1901, p. 138. See also *Bouche de Fer*, 4 July 1791, No. 82, pp. 1–7; 10 July 1791, No. 88, pp. 3–7.

[2] *Révolutions de Paris*, 7–14 May 1791, No. 96, p. 253 ff.

[3] Aulard, *La Société des Jacobins*, 1889–97, II, 573–4. See also *Opinion de P. F. Réal sur la question de savoir quel parti il faut prendre*, etc., *prononcé le 3 juillet.*

[4] Robert, *Le républicanisme*, etc., 1790; Anon., *Le despotisme décrété par l'Assemblée Nationale*, 1790; Billaud-Varenne, *L'Acéphrocatie* etc., 1791.

this journal, ceased. The last reference was in the issue of 25 June, when his definition of the word 'republic' was discussed and said to be misleading.[1]

It is of course true that members of every revolutionary faction appealed to Rousseau's name at some stage or other, but Aulard rightly infers that in so far as the republicans did use Rousseau's name it was in order to strengthen views of which they were already convinced, rather than as that of the prophet to whom they owed their inspiration.

(iii) *Federalism*

A number of writers referred to Rousseau's name in the course of arguments about federalism, but it would be difficult to prove, on the basis of these references, that Rousseau's theories inspired a federalist movement between 1789 and 1791. For the abbé Fauchet[2] and the journalist Mercier[3] federalism was the means whereby French predominance and the dissemination of revolutionary ideas throughout Europe could be achieved. Both held, contrary to Rousseau's view, which they rejected, that it was possible to establish just laws and institutions in all societies, regardless of geographical divergences or of history. Gudin appreciated that for Rousseau federalism was the means whereby the independence of small states could be secured, but he devoted a chapter of his book on the *Social Contract* to rejecting the ideal of the small state.[4] Billaud-Varenne proposed the establishment of a federal republic in France, but he seems to have been unaware that Rousseau held views on federalism at all. Although he quoted from the *Dedication* to the *Second Discourse* to support his views on sovereignty, he made no reference to the *Social Contract*, or to the *Considérations sur le gouvernement de Pologne* or to the *Jugement sur la paix perpétuelle*, in which Rousseau expressed his views on federalism.[5]

I have discovered only one clear example of Rousseau's

[1] *Bouche de Fer*, 25 June 1791, No. 73, p. 3.
[2] Ibid. Dec. 1790, No. XXXI, p. 484 ff. See also Ch. VI.
[3] Mercier, 1791, II, vi, 65 ff.
[4] Gudin, *Supplément*, etc., 1790, Part II, ch. ix, p. 68 ff.
[5] Billaud-Varenne, *L'Acéphrocatie*, etc., 1791.

theories having inspired a demand for a federal type of government. This was in 1792 when Terasson proposed in the Jacobin Club that instead of discussing the best type of government for France they should simply discuss federalism, because Rousseau had said that federalism was the best form of government for any society. This proposal appears to have been met with scorn and some impatience. It was pointed out in reply that if they wanted to establish a federation they would have to begin, as Rousseau himself had perceived, by burning Paris.[1]

In these circumstances, d'Antraigues, who claimed that he destroyed Rousseau's manuscript on federalism with which the author had entrusted him, because he feared the uses to which it might be put, seems to have given himself needless trouble.[2]

(iv) *Socialism*

Both Taine[3] and Louis Blanc[4] regarded Rousseau as having inspired socialistic ideas during the Revolution. It is necessary to remember that the idea that extreme inequality was harmful to society and contrary to natural law is one which runs through much of the philosophy of the eighteenth century. Not only Rousseau, but Morelly, Mably and Helvétius condemned the corrupting influence of wealth and the evils of property,[5] as the journal *Révolutions de Paris* pointed out.[6] Secondly, it must be remembered that during the early years of the Revolution it seemed to many democratically-minded Frenchmen that a new aristocracy of wealth was being established with a monopoly of government at both the national and local levels. Two admirers of Rousseau advocated a more

[1] Aulard, *La Société des Jacobins*, 1889–97, IV, p. 273 ff. Terasson's proposal was refuted by Chaleot.

[2] D'Antraigues, *Quelle est la situation*, etc.?, 1790. Compare Vaughan, II, and Cobban, *Rousseau and the modern state*, 1964, appendix I.

[3] Taine, *L'Ancien Régime*, pp. 289–301, 322.

[4] See Ch. II.

[5] See Morelly, *Code de la nature*; Helvétius, *De l'homme*, sect. VI, chs. iii to v, on the corrupting effects of luxury, *Œuvres*, IV; also *Lettres de Montesquieu*, *Œuvres*, V, 215 ff.; Mably, *L'Étude de l'Histoire*, p. 369 ff., in which the author discusses the *loi agraire*.

[6] *Révolutions de Paris*, 7–14 March 1791, No. 96, p. 243. The authority of the philosophers was invoked in reply to La Harpe, who, in an article in the *Mercure*, 23 April 1791, had attacked the article 'Les Pauvres et les Riches'. See n. 2 below.

equitable distribution of land among the people as a means of breaking this monopoly. Gudin, a moderate constitutional monarchist, was a shrewd analyst of the forces at work in 1790; he perceived the precariousness of the new revolutionary government and he wished to stabilize the foundations of the constitution by extending the number of property holders in the state.[1] Loustalot urged the more equal distribution of property and a wider participation in government because he wished to break down the political monopoly of the new aristocracy of wealth in Paris.[2] Both these writers, though they referred to Rousseau's theories, were inspired not by Rousseau's works but by their practical appraisal of the political situation. Neither were in the true sense socialists; they did not attack property, on the contrary they recognized property as the basis of citizenship; they attacked only its unequal distribution. This was a point frequently made in the long debates about the confiscation of church property and the principle was in fact recognized by the law of 14 May 1790.

During the interesting and important debate in the Constituent Assembly on the nationalization and sale of church property, several protagonists of the scheme, notably Talleyrand and Thouret, urged that it should ensure an increase in the number of landowners as well as bring much-needed financial relief to the state. Their advocacy bore fruit in the decree of 14 May 1790 which was the basis of the entire operation. Its preamble specifically stated that one of its purposes was 'l'accroissement heureux . . . du nombre des propriétaires' and the regulations provided that bids for nationalized lands were to be accepted for the whole or for parts of a lot simultaneously, and that when the total number of bids for parts of a lot were equal to a bid for the whole, the former were to have preference.[3]

The abbé Fauchet was accused by Anarcharsis Cloots of having advocated a 'loi agraire' in 1790 because he stated,

[1] Gudin, *Supplément*, etc., 1790, III, ch. v, p. 110 ff.

[2] *Révolutions de Paris*, 29 January–5 February 1791, No. 82. See 'Les Pauvres et les Riches'; also, 7–14 March 1791, No. 96, *Réponse à des observations de M. de la Harpe*, etc., p. 242 ff.

[3] *Mon. Réimp.*, II, 37–8, 84; L. Cahen and R. Guyot, *L'Œuvre législative de la Révolution française*, 1913, pp. 404–8, for the text of the decree.

during the course of a lecture on Rousseau, that in an ideal society all property would be communal.[1] Fauchet was clearly rather startled by this accusation. He had in fact been preaching the redistribution of property since 1789 at least, and no one had ever assumed that he was speaking other than theoretically. He pointed this out; he was, he said, only stating Rousseau's principles. In practice he fully acknowledged that an attempt to divide property would result in anarchy.[2] Fauchet was not normally a speaker who allowed practical considerations to inhibit his oratory. His inspiration was religious rather than philosophical and his addiction to economic equality preceded his addiction to Rousseau.[3]

(v) *The Civil Constitution of the Clergy*

Jules Lemaître asserted that this was derived from Book IV, Ch. VIII of the *Social Contract*,[4] but there seems to be no evidence to support his contention. I have found only one reference to Rousseau's name in relation to the civil constitution. This is in an article by Daunou, originally published in the *Journal Encyclopédique* in 1790, and Daunou, although in favour of the civil constitution, disapproves of Rousseau's arguments in the *Social Contract*.[5]

(vi) *The system of 'gradual elections'*

It is curious that historians attempting to show the importance of Rousseau's influence should have overlooked the one occasion when a proposal put before the Assembly can be shown to have been lifted directly from the pages of one of his works.

On 10 December 1789, Mirabeau made a speech advocating

[1] See *Bouche de Fer*, 14 April 1791, No. 42, pp. 103–14.

[2] Ibid. p. 108. For Fauchet's views on property see also *Bouche de Fer*, Nov. 1790, No. XXII, p. 347, and J. Charrier, *Claude Fauchet: Évêque constitutionnel de Calvados*, 1909.

[3] See Fauchet, *La Religion nationale*, 1789, sections III, IV, V, p. 323 ff.

[4] Lemaître, *Jean-Jacques Rousseau*, see p. 278.

[5] Daunou, 'De la religion publique, etc.', *L'Esprit des Journaux*, April, 1790, p. 222 ff.

that the promotion of civil officers should be regulated in accordance with their periods of service in a subordinate capacity. Thus no citizen could be elected to the council of a department unless he had first served on a municipal council, and no citizen would become a candidate for the National Assembly without having either sat on the council of a department or held public office for two years. This speech had been drafted by Étienne Dumont, who recounts in his *Souvenirs sur Mirabeau* how he first came upon the idea in the *Considérations*. Dumont believed that the authority of Rousseau's name, coupled with an appeal to the traditions of Rome and Geneva, would prove irresistible. Mirabeau's speech was, indeed, applauded; the idea was taken up by Roederer and Clermont-Tonnerre, both of whom spoke in its favour. There, however, Dumont's triumph ended. Barnave and the Lameths condemned the idea as aristocratic, and it was rejected by the Assembly. Dumont was annoyed with Mirabeau for having lost interest in the project so quickly when faced with opposition; Mirabeau enjoyed the applause earned by a brilliant speech, he said, but was not prepared to study the subject in the detail required to defend it from serious criticism in the course of debate.[1] It was left to Dumont himself to reply to the criticisms of Barnave, which he did in a series of articles in the *Courrier de Provence*.[2]

In these articles the authority of Rousseau was quickly passed over, the author's main interest being to score against Barnave the points which Mirabeau had failed to make in debate. It is clear that as far as the Assembly was concerned, the Rousseauist inspiration of this proposal carried very little weight. As for Dumont himself, he was not strictly speaking influenced by Rousseau, but was casting about for a suitable subject on which Mirabeau might exercise his oratorical powers. He continued to argue his case because, as he complained, Mirabeau had failed to do it justice.[3]

[1] Etienne Dumont, *Souvenirs sur Mirabeau*, ed. J. Bénétruy, 1951, pp. 139–40. Mirabeau's speech is given in the appendix to an earlier edition of the *Souvenirs*, ed. Duval, 1832.

[2] *Courrier de Provence*, 9–10 Dec. 1789, No. LXXVII, 16 Dec. 1789, No. LXXIX.

[3] The debates on this subject were recorded in the *Mon. Réimp.* for 10 and 15 Dec. 1789, Nos. 111 and 115. The original sources were the *Journal des Débats*, *Le Hodey* and the *Courrier de Provence*.

General References to Rousseau's Name and Works

Finally, an analysis of the references to Rousseau in the pamphlets of the period 1789 to 1791 reveals strikingly the vagueness with which his name was used. His authority was commonly invoked, without reference to his works, to add weight to purely personal views and to opinions which were diametrically opposite to his own. Pamphleteers and orators frequently appealed not to one authority but to many, and associated a variety of philosophers, often most unsuitably, in support of their projects, regardless of the views which these adopted heroes of the Revolution had expressed in their own life-times. Thus Rousseau's name was associated with those of Voltaire, Montesquieu, Raynal and Mably, to say nothing of Benjamin Franklin, Bacon, Sidney and Locke.

It is difficult to make any survey of a statistical nature of the references to Rousseau's name and works. Any such evidence must inevitably be incomplete. In the first place, the amount of material is too great to permit an exhaustive study; in the second, the evidence arising from such a survey cannot be regarded as representative of the whole body of revolutionary literature for the period. The student must to a certain extent be selective, and must be led, both by specific references and reasonable supposition, to particular pamphlets and particular writers. Thus an analysis of the pamphlets read during the course of this study would be heavily weighted in favour of those writers who expounded, or purported to expound, the theories of Rousseau, and would therefore tend to over-estimate Rousseau's influence. A good deal of time has however been spent in a more or less random search for references to Rousseau's name and works in collections of pamphlets published between 1788 and 1791 which are available in the British Museum, and the statistical survey which follows is put forward as a tentative indication. Of the seven references to 'other works' which are listed, five were to *Émile* and two to the *Dedication to the Second Discourse*.

This survey is clearly of limited range, but it is of interest within its limitations since it bears out the conclusions reached so far in this study, that the importance attached to Rousseau's political influence has been greatly exaggerated.

A. Pamphlets relating to the Estates General

British Museum references	Total no. of pamphlets	References to Rousseau: Social contract	Other works	General	Total no. of references
FR 9–21 FR 42–48	222 181 } 403	6	3	2	11
R 50–53	69	1	0	2	3
F 23–24	21	0	0	3	3
FR 14	20	1	0	0	1
Total	513	8	3	7	18

B. Pamphlets relating to the National and Constituent Assemblies

British Museum references	Total no. of pamphlets	References to Rousseau: Social contract	Other works	General	Total no. of references
R 69–77	181	0	0	5	5
R 560	22	0	0	0	0
FR 33	36	0	0	2	2
FR 76	26	0	0	0	0
Total	265	0	0	7	7

C. Pamphlets relating to the Paris Clubs

A

British Museum references	Total no. of pamphlets	References to Rousseau: Social contract	Other works	General	Total no. of references
FR 366	28	0	0	0	0
R 157/8	45	0	0	0	0
R 340/1/2	14	1	0	1	2
F 333/45	30	0	0	0	0
F 338/9	5	1	0	0	1
F 343/4	23	0	2	0	2
F 345/16	11	0	0	0	0
F 347/48	19	0	0	1	1
F 349/50	5	0	0	0	0
F 351/2/3	5	0	0	0	0
F 354/5	9	0	0	0	0
F 356/7	3	0	0	0	0
F 336/7	19	0	0	0	0
	216	2	2	2	6
B	Journal of the Jacobin Club				
F 89*–90*	120 (June 1790–Dec. 1791)	2	2	4	8
Total	1,114	12	7	20	39

CHAPTER VI

The Exposition of Rousseau's Political Theory, 1788–1791

PROBABLY the most widely read of all the pamphlets on the subject of the convocation of the Estates General, until the publication of the more famous *Qu'est-ce que le Tiers État* of the abbé Sieyès, was d'Antraigues' *Mémoire sur les États Généraux.*[1] Published in November 1788, a second edition appeared before the end of the year, and a third early in 1789. In two respects this pamphlet was typical of the period. D'Antraigues made a study of the historical development of the Estates General and traced the principle of popular sovereignty to the actual exercise of sovereign rights by the people in the early history of France. On the other hand the pamphlet was unique because d'Antraigues also appealed to fundamental political principles, which he discussed at some length and which were almost certainly derived from the *Social Contract.*

D'Antraigues was an admirer of Rousseau, whom, as a young man, he had personally known. He later claimed that Rousseau had entrusted to him the draft of a treatise which he intended as a sequel to the *Social Contract.*[2] In this pamphlet he did not in fact mention Rousseau by name, although he referred indirectly to the great philosopher. This in itself is interesting as suggesting that the appeal to Rousseau's authority in political controversy was a less obvious expedient in 1788 for commanding attention than it subsequently became. Nevertheless the

[1] See p. 5, n. 2 above.

[2] *Quelle est la situation de l'Assemblée Nationale?*, 1790, pp. 30, 31, n. 1. See p. 59, n. 2 above and p. 122, n. 1 below.

first part of d'Antraigues' pamphlet reads like a summary of the first three books of the *Social Contract.*

The pamphlet is divided into two parts. In the first part d'Antraigues dealt with what he regarded as the fundamental principles of political right, which, he insisted, were constant, immutable and universally applicable. The main principles he stated were: the inalienable sovereignty of the people and the consequent limitation of the function of elected deputies; the necessity of a division of function between legislative and executive; and finally the principle that he who draws up the constitution must not exercise political power under it. In the second and longest part of his pamphlet d'Antraigues attempted to show, by a study of French history, how these principles had in fact been fundamental to the French constitution, although obscured by the growth of feudalism and tyranny. Whenever the Estates General had met, he claimed, these principles had been re-asserted by the deputies of the people, and more recently, in the absence of the Estates, by the Parlements.

D'Antraigues emphasized most strongly, and this was the most important argument in his thesis, that the inalienable sovereignty of the people had been recognized throughout French history by the insistence on the part of the peoples' deputies that they were bound by an imperative mandate, which limited their powers simply to the role of expressing the will of their constituents. It was the imperative mandate, buttressed by the Rousseauist concept of inalienable sovereignty, which he put forward as the essential and traditional basis for the regeneration of the state. By 'regeneration' he meant, in fact, a return to the purer political principles of the past, though the past which he created for France was largely imaginary.

Although he ostensibly put forward the theory of the mandate as the means whereby the rights of the nation could best be protected from the despotic power of the administration, in effect he was putting forward a plan by which the hands of the deputies would be bound; owing to the necessity of abiding by the instructions of their constituents they would be unable to initiate legislation as a result of deliberation and discussion among themselves. D'Antraigues did not even allow for the regular convening of the Estates by law. He thought that this should be left to the discretion of the king. Thus Rousseau's theory of inalienable sovereignty was launched into the sphere of political controversy in association with a theory of the state which was fundamentally conservative. Presented as the logical conclusion to the practical recognition of the sovereignty of the people and as the means of protecting the people's deputies from the blandishments of the executive, the aristocratic character of the 'mandat impératif' was not immediately clear. D'Antraigues' association of the concept of the mandate with the principle of popular sovereignty was, indeed, a unique contribution to the political thought of 1788.

D'Antraigues also put forward a theory of recurrent national regeneration through violence, which can be recognized as a development of certain ideas expressed in the *Social Contract*. Rousseau had stated that there were times in the history of states when violence and civil war had the effect of reinvigorating a people, so that the state rose again, like the phoenix from its ashes, and reassumed the vigour of youth.[1] He also pointed out that peace and tranquillity did not always ensure human happiness, observing that Odysseus' men no doubt lived very tranquilly while waiting for the Cyclops to eat them.[2] These arguments were, however, more in the nature of asides to the logical development of Rousseau's main argument. He emphasized that states had their own life cycles, and that the regeneration of a state was so rare as to be exceptional. Such an event could only happen to a people which was still young and vigorous. Both in the *Social Contract* and in his advice to the King of Poland, Rousseau emphasized that a people with a long history would be more likely to find a master than a liberator in revolution.[3]

Since the idea of regeneration was very much 'in the air' at the time when d'Antraigues was writing, it is perhaps not entirely surprising that he should have placed his emphasis on what, to Rousseau, had been the least important aspect of his

[1] *C.S.*, II, ch. viii, Vaughan, II, 55. See also III, ch. iv, n., Vaughan, II, 88.

[2] Ibid. I, ch. iv, Vaughan, II, 28. This analogy was borrowed by Rousseau from Locke's *Second Treatise*.

[3] Ibid. II, ch. viii, Vaughan, II, 55. See also *C.G.P.*, Vaughan, II, 445.

argument. At the beginning of his pamphlet d'Antraigues stated, in words reminiscent of the analogy used by Rousseau:

. . . toujours juste. . . . Dieu permit qu'au fort de leur oppression il existât pour les peuples asservis un moyen de se régénérer et de reprendre l'éclat de la jeunesse en sortant des bras de la mort.[1]

He then proceeded to develop the theory that the very excesses of tyranny brought about its own destruction, and that in the violence of war and the shedding of blood, the virtues of honour and courage were born again in the individual. These became the basis for a regenerated social order. While, therefore, d'Antraigues adopted Rousseau's view that states had their periods of infancy, virility and senility, he apparently believed that this life cycle was a recurrent process in each state.

Thus, in his *Mémoire*, d'Antraigues launched two main arguments which he derived from the *Social Contract* and adapted to his own prejudices and to those of his times. While his debt to the *Social Contract* is clear, it is less clear that his pamphlet can be regarded as an important medium for spreading Rousseauist ideas, or drawing the attention of its many readers to Rousseau's political theory, and to the *Social Contract* in particular. As already pointed out, Rousseau's name was not actually mentioned in the pamphlet, and there is no reason to suppose that in 1788 and 1789 familiarity with the *Social Contract* was so widespread that d'Antraigues' readers would recognize the Rousseauist origins of his argument. Moreover, the pamphlet, though widely read in 1788 and in the early months of 1789, received its death blow from the meeting of the Estates General. It could not survive when once the breach between aristocratic and democratic opinion had been made explicit in relation to the practical issues of procedure. The argument between the two factions tore through the whole fabric of d'Antraigues' thesis, uniting as it did the theory of the sovereignty of the people with that of the imperative mandate. The aristocracy could not, in practice, recognize the former, while the democrats could not, in practice, accept the latter. The combination of the two theories was indeed to be a source of continued

[1] *Mémoire sur les États Généraux*, etc., p. 1.

embarrassment to subsequent exponents of Rousseau's political thought, both revolutionary and aristocratic, since one or other had to be explained away according to the point of view of the writer. In the light of subsequent developments it became clear that the theory which d'Antraigues was putting forward was essentially aristocratic.

D'Antraigues himself lost the favour of the Third Estate in the summer of 1789 by his defence of the traditional procedure of deliberation and vote by order, to which the aristocratic deputies argued that they were bound by their mandates. It is interesting to observe, that in the many arguments which he put forward in defence of the imperative mandate during June and July of 1789, both in the *Chambre de la Noblesse*, and as a member of the commission appointed by the nobles to meet members of the Third Estate, he did not appeal, as he had done in his pamphlet, to the theory of inalienable popular sovereignty. Like his aristocratic colleagues, he justified the imperative mandate by appealing to the traditional rights of the ancient orders, and to the precedents of earlier Estates General.[1]

Finally, d'Antraigues' pamphlet cannot be regarded as of any great importance as a means whereby the popular idea of regeneration could have been specifically associated with Rousseau's name. The word 'regeneration' was on the lips and pens of so many orators and writers from 1788 onward, that d'Antraigues may be regarded as writing in the language of his times rather than as spreading a new idea culled from the pages of the *Social Contract*. It is true that the idea of regeneration came to be associated particularly with the name of Rousseau in the revolutionary cult, but it will be shown that this association was derived from the personal legend of Rousseau as a great moral teacher and not from the *Social Contract*.[2] D'Antraigues' pamphlet is illustrative of the way in which the interpretation of Rousseau's text was affected by current political ideas, rather than the reverse.

During 1788–89 three other works specifically relating to

[1] D'Antraigues put forward his views on the imperative mandate in a series of speeches during the course of 1789. These are listed, with dates and references, in the bibliography below.

[2] This distinction is discussed in Ch. XII.

Rousseau's political theories were published. The authors of two of these were conservative in outlook. The Jesuit Berthier had begun a detailed examination and criticism of the text of the *Social Contract* in 1762, immediately after its publication. When the *Social Contract* was officially condemned, Berthier abandoned his project which he regarded as having now become superfluous. In 1789 an unknown author, possibly the abbé Bourdier Delpuito, undertook to complete and edit the work at the request of Berthier's publishers. It finally appeared under the title *Observations sur le Contrat Social de J. J. Rousseau.*

In 1789 there also appeared a lengthy pamphlet by a M. Isnard entitled *Le principe qui a produit les Révolutions de France, de Genève et d'Amérique dans le dix-huitième siècle.* This consisted mainly of an attack on the Rousseauist principles of the general will. Isnard argued that Rousseau had put forward a theory of law based on the tyrannical and irrational will of the majority, and that the theory of the revolutionaries was lifted from the pages of the *Social Contract*, replacing the traditional concept of law as the expression of divine and universal reason. He wrote:

> Le Contrat Social contient le dangereux principe qui a produit les révolutions de la patrie de J. J. Rousseau, qui a enlevé l'Amérique à l'Angleterre, qui peut enlever la France à la maison de Bourbon et qui peut-être, pour les malheurs de l'Europe, fermentera encore longtemps dans les têtes agitées par quelques teintures de politique. . . . Voici le fatal principe qui a entrainé les Genèvois, les Américains et les Français:
>
> La loi est l'acte ou l'expression de la volonté générale.[1]

The publication in 1789 of these two works attacking Rousseau's political thought is significant, and appears at first sight to be at variance with the lack of evidence that the *Social Contract* was widely read in 1789. It is, however, possible that those who believed it necessary, in 1789, to attack what seemed to be the growing influence of Rousseau's political theory may have been labouring under the same misapprehension which has misled some later historians. That is to say that interest in Rousseau as the prophet and patron of the Revolution was

[1] Isnard, *Le principe qui a produit les révolutions*, etc., 1789, p. 1.

taken as evidence of the influence of the *Social Contract* and current political ideas of a revolutionary or democratic nature were therefore ascribed to that work, and fathered upon Rousseau.

It is impossible to ascertain how far this is true by studying Berthier's text, since Berthier, writing in 1762, could not have been affected by the ideas current in 1789. His study, a very detailed and scholarly criticism, was limited severely to the text of the *Social Contract*. Nevertheless, what he wrote in 1762 does not disprove the suggestion put forward above as to why his book was published in 1789. Moreover, a study of Isnard's pamphlet bears this argument out, for Isnard was in fact concerned to attack not the theories of the *Social Contract* but the theories of the Revolution, which he took to be those of Rousseau. Although Isnard wrote about the general will, he did not write about the general will as Rousseau used the expression. On the contrary, he directed his criticisms against the idea that the laws should be based on the will of the majority, and assumed that this revolutionary concept was derived from the *Social Contract*. It is hardly necessary to point out that Rousseau himself had been careful to distinguish between the general will and the will of the majority. Moreover, there is no reason to suppose that the revolutionaries derived the expression from the *Social Contract*. Other writers besides Rousseau made use of it, and by 1789 it had passed into the general vocabulary of politics.

Further enquiry may help us to substantiate or reject this interpretation of the books of d'Antraigues, Berthier and Isnard.

When we come to consider the exposition of Rousseau's work by writers whose sympathies were with the Revolution we find a very great diversity of interpretation. No pamphlets specifically bearing on Rousseau's political thought, and written from a revolutionary point of view, appear to have been published in 1788. In 1789 one pamphlet appeared, consisting of a series of extracts from the *Social Contract*, carefully selected to give the impression that nothing Rousseau wrote conflicted with popular revolutionary ideology.[1] It was not

[1] Anon., *J. J. Rousseau des Champs Élysées à la Nation française*, 1789.

until 1790 that a work devoted to showing the relation between the development of the Revolution and the theory of Rousseau was published. This was the *Supplément au Contrat Social, applicable particulièrement aux grandes nations*, by Paul Philippe Gudin de Brenellerie.

Gudin was better known during his own lifetime as a dramatist than as a political theorist, but in 1789 he won a prize awarded by the Académie Française for his *Essai sur l'histoire des comices de Rome, des États Généraux de France et du Parlement d'Angleterre*. This was followed in 1790 by the *Supplément*, which he addressed to the Constituent Assembly.

The work appears to have been fairly widely read, as further editions appeared in 1791 and 1792. Gudin was a constitutional monarchist who, even by 1790, had become uneasy at the activities of those whom he regarded as extremists in the National Assembly. While, therefore, he eulogized the achievements of 1789, his exposition of Rousseau's principles was fundamentally conservative in relation to the France of 1790. His main interest was to safeguard the independence of the executive by preserving the royal power of veto, and to restrain those restless spirits who wanted to carry the Revolution further. During the Terror the *Supplément* was proscribed for its monarchist leanings and Gudin himself fled.

He began by stating the ideal principles contained in the *Social Contract* and by showing how these could be applied in a small republic; he then demonstrated their inapplicability in a large state. How, he asked, could liberty be retained in a large state? The essence of Rousseau's theory, he decided, was the concept of law as an expression of the general will, and the problem of the great state was to combine the representative system with the legislative supremacy of the general will. Rousseau had in fact denied that such a combination was possible. Gudin admitted that it was difficult. One of the few writers to understand Rousseau's use of the expression *volonté générale*, he was also acutely aware of the dangers of representation. It was from the representative assembly, which he thought inevitably attracted the dissatisfied, the personally ambitious, and those with a gift for swaying crowds, that in Gudin's view the main danger of particularist legislation came.

An admirer of the English constitution, he therefore proposed that all legislation originating in the National Assembly should be submitted to an upper house, which would be representative of the more conservative elements of society. He did not describe the constitution of this house very clearly, but he seems to have visualized something similar to the American Senate, to which members would be elected to sit for a longer period than in the lower house. Secondly, he proposed that all legislation passing through both houses should be subject to the royal veto. By this practical division of the legislative power into three sections he hoped that the urge toward innovation would always be tempered by the voices of custom and moderation, and that in this way the general will would be expressed.

Thus in attempting to apply Rousseau's principles to France in 1789, Gudin reached a very different position from that of Rousseau himself. Beginning with the Rousseauist principle that law is the expression of the general will, he finally arrived at a completely unrousseauist position by dividing the sovereign into three. Gudin was, of course, aware of the difficulties of his task. There is a certain dualism in his attitude to the *Social Contract*. In the opening chapters of the *Supplément* in which he examined Rousseau's principles, he was clearly carried away by the ideal of the small republic; on the other hand, in the last part of the book, in which he examined revolutionary France, he was equally carried away by enthusiasm for the achievements of 1789, and showed some scorn for Rousseau's predilection for small states. Because of this dualism and because of Gudin's own uneasiness as to the future development of the Revolution, it is difficult to generalize about his attitude towards either Rousseau or the Revolution. Nevertheless, Gudin's work showed greater scholarship, integrity and understanding of Rousseau's meaning than the majority of revolutionary tracts. His admission that discrepancies existed between the theory of the *Social Contract* and the possible organization of a country the size of France was a remarkable conclusion for a revolutionary exponent of Rousseauism, and one which earned him much hostile criticism.[1]

[1] See p. 81, n. 1 below.

In the following year Louis Sebastien Mercier published his well known *De J. J. Rousseau considéré comme l'un des premiers auteurs de la Révolution*. Mercier, like Gudin, was a dramatist and literary critic, with keen political interests; he was the author of the *Tableau de Paris* and between 1788 and 1793 collaborated in producing a complete edition of Rousseau's works.[1] His own most important work, published in 1778, was *De la littérature et des littérateurs*. Mercier knew Rousseau personally during the latter's last years, and his book on Rousseau has been much quoted as an authoritative assessment of Rousseau's political influence. An examination of this work is, however, disconcerting. In the first place, it is difficult to understand how any intelligent reader could interpret the *Social Contract* in the sense in which Mercier apparently interprets it, even in the excitement of a political upheaval on the scale of the French Revolution. Secondly, it is difficult to see how his book could be used as evidence to support the argument that the *Social Contract* was widely read or closely studied by the revolutionaries. Mercier himself admitted that the *Social Contract* had in fact been of all Rousseau's works the least read up to 1791. In making this statement he involved himself in a contradiction, for his main purpose was to establish the importance of Rousseau's influence as a political thinker, and particularly of the *Social Contract*. If, as he maintained, this work was not widely read prior to 1791, then the question arises how knowledge of Rousseau's political theory was transmitted. One fact is clear: knowledge of Rousseau's political theory was certainly not transmitted after 1791 through the media of Mercier's pages.

His interpretation of Rousseau's political thought can only lead to the conclusion that either he had not read the *Social Contract* or that, if he had read it, he had forgotten or totally misunderstood its contents. Two striking examples of his misinterpretation of Rousseau's ideas may be quoted. Mercier states categorically that it was Rousseau's view that a people, to be free, must give itself representatives,[2] and he describes Rousseau's view of the state as a mechanism, in which the

[1] See Vaughan, II, 13. Mercier's associates in editing Rousseau's works were G. Brizzard and F. H. S. de l'Aulnaye.

[2] Mercier, *J. J. Rousseau*, etc., 1791, II, v, 7, 8.

liberty of the subject is secured only by a perpetual conflict between the independent branches of government, each struggling for dominion over the others.[1] These are fantastic contradictions of what Rousseau actually said.

Among the revolutionary exponents of Rousseauism, Claude Fauchet has probably the distinction of being the most colourful, if not the most accurate. As abbé of Montfort-Lacane, he took a leading part in the storming of the Bastille, narrowly escaping death. On subsequent occasions, at meetings of the *Cercle Social* he proudly wore the surplice which had been torn by bullets on that memorable 14th July. Fauchet was elected in 1789 to represent the district of Saint-Roche as a deputy to the Paris Commune. In May 1791 he was appointed Constitutional Bishop of Calvados, and represented this department in the Legislative Assembly and the Convention. In July 1793 he was denounced by Chabot for his association with the Gironde and as an accomplice of Charlotte Corday. He was executed in the following October.

Between October 1790 and April 1791 Fauchet delivered a series of discourses on the *Social Contract* to the members of the *Cercle Social des Amis de la Vérité*. This rather curious society originated as a Masonic lodge. Its founder, Nicholas Bonneville, believed that the ideals of freemasonry and those of the Revolution were identical, that is, the regeneration of human kind and the universal brotherhood of man. To Fauchet these views were by no means irreconcilable with Christianity. He regarded the Revolution as an apocalyptic event, a stage in the divine plan for the progressive revelation of truth. Human society had now at last reached the stage in which perfectibility was possible. The truths revealed through the Revolution to the French people must be revealed to the peoples of other nations. It was the aim of the *Cercle Social* to establish a network of branches or lodges throughout France, and gradually to extend these beyond the frontiers. These cells would propagate the true principles of political philosophy; they would form the centres from which the regenerating power would operate; ultimately they would form the nucleus of a universal federation of peoples.

[1] Ibid. II. v, 89 ff.

These ideas were given expression in the organ of the *Cercle Social*, the *Bouche de Fer*,[1] of which Fauchet and Nicholas Bonneville were co-editors and chief contributors. Needless to say, they aroused a good deal of ridicule.[2] Fauchet's religious enthusiasm and his Panglossian faith in universal natural harmony were palpably unreal even by the optimistic standards of his contemporaries.

Fauchet's discourses on the *Social Contract* were attended by a great variety of people, although, as might be expected, the numbers declined. Among those who listened to his inaugural address were Sieyès, Condorcet, Mme. Roland, Brissot, Camille Desmoulins and Tom Paine. Oratory rather than discussion was characteristic of these sessions and there is very little record of the reactions of the audience, except for the frequent references to applause. It is therefore difficult to discover how far Fauchet aroused interest in Rousseau's theories, as distinct from his own, or whether any further study of the *Social Contract* resulted from his discourses. Fauchet did not so much discuss Rousseau's theories as put forward his own: strictly speaking he did not set out to instruct his listeners in the principles of the *Social Contract* but rather to use Rousseau's text as a starting point for the exposition of his own views. Nor was he uncritical of Rousseau. At the beginning of his series of lectures he announced that his aim was to discover that true system of legislation which could be applied to all men, and that the *Social Contract* was to provide the basis for this enquiry. This remark was greeted with applause, whereupon Fauchet warned his listeners against a blind adulation of Rousseau, who, he said, had been guilty of many absurdities.[3] His attitude to Rousseau was rather patronizing; Rousseau spoke, he believed,

[1] After May 1791, Bonneville alone directed the *Bouche de Fer*, the publication of which was suspended after No. 104, 28 July 1791.

[2] See, for example, *Révolutions de Paris*, 30 Oct.–6 Nov. 1790, No. 69, p. 176 ff.; Charrier, *Claude Fauchet*, etc., pp. 170–1. Fauchet was also attacked by La Harpe, see *Correspondance Littéraire*, IV, let. 293, p. 186, and by Cloots, see *Courier des Départements*, 24 Oct. 1790. See also an article in the *Mercure de France*, 18 Dec. 1790, in which Fauchet's plans for universal brotherhood were ridiculed. Members of the Jacobin Club were extremely hostile to Fauchet whom they accused of attacking property. In Nov. 1790 they accepted a motion of Laclos that all affiliated societies should be warned not to associate with the *Cercle Social*.

[3] *Bouche de Fer*, Oct. 1790, No. XI, pp. 167–8.

from an age of darkness, before the Revolution had clarified men's minds, and his vision was inevitably distorted by pessimism. They would therefore adopt, Fauchet decided, those principles which were in keeping with their purpose and reject whatever was in contradiction with it, assuming that in such cases Rousseau had been wrong. Although on some occasions, for example in his criticism of Rousseau's chapter on the different forms of government suitable to different types of country, he took the text of the *Social Contract* paragraph by paragraph,[1] he more frequently dispensed with it altogether. In his tenth discourse, in which he showed how the people of a great nation could exercise sovereignty with wisdom and ease, he omitted all reference to Rousseau.[2] Unless his hearers had been already familiar with the *Social Contract*, they would not have learned a great deal about Rousseau's political thought from Fauchet, except in very general terms, nor could they easily have distinguished between Rousseau's views and those of Fauchet himself.

How far, in fact, did Fauchet find himself in agreement with the *Social Contract*? The very purpose of his discourses shows a fundamental cleavage between his own views and those which Rousseau had held. Fauchet believed that it was possible to formulate principles of government which could be universally applied.[3] The *Social Contract* was criticized both during and before the Revolution for being too abstract, but Fauchet criticized it for precisely the opposite fault, charging Rousseau with having paid too much attention to details of geography and economics and to the differences arising from custom and history. These factors Fauchet dismissed as irrelevant. All human beings were part of a universal, divine, natural pattern. To assert that material factors such as geography or economics, or the accidents of history might necessitate different forms of government, or even, in some circumstances, preclude good government altogether, was to Fauchet nothing short of blasphemous. Fauchet, unlike Rousseau, was an optimist. He believed in progress. Once the people were enlightened and

[1] Ibid. 25 March 1791, No. 35, pp. 549–60.
[2] Ibid. Oct. 1790, No. III, p. 18.
[3] Ibid. Oct. 1790, No. III, p. 18.

taught their rights, corruption and despotism would never again raise their heads. The French people had reached this maturity, but their example eould be followed by other peoples, less politically developed, for once the principles of the Revolution were generally made known, the peoples of other nations would recognize them as the principles of natural right.

Finally, Fauchet differed from Rousseau in his whole concept of sovereignty. At first sight he appears to approach more nearly to the Rousseauist concept of the general will than many of his contemporaries. This is because he believed the general will to be based on man's moral goodness. However, this likeness is superficial, for Fauchet derived his concept of the general will from premises directly contrary to those assumed by Rousseau. He held that men were naturally sociable and good; indeed the two words are interchangeable in his philosophy. He specifically rejected Rousseau's distinction between social and natural man, and his description of the latter as amoral and non-social. Fauchet, in opposition to Rousseau, held that society must inevitably become good because the will that shaped it was based on man's natural goodness and therefore intrinsically altruistic. Again, when it came to the question of how the general will could be recognized, Fauchet took the conventional view and simply equated it with the will of the majority.

Fauchet had been one of the most vociferous critics of representation during 1789–90, but here again it would be a mistake to assume that he was speaking as a disciple of Rousseau. In the first place, he did not derive his views from the *Social Contract*, but used, curiously enough, theological arguments to justify the submission of legislation to primary assemblies of electors.[1] Secondly, Fauchet was critical of Rousseau's outright condemnation of representation, since he believed that representatives played a very important part in the political education of the people, in so far as they clarified the people's minds. Fauchet had no hesitation in declaring that the general will was ex-

[1] In the pamphlet *Sur les droits des représentants et du peuple*, 1789, Fauchet argued that God did not promulgate laws until they had been 'sanctioned' by the other heavenly inhabitants. Fauchet's views on popular sanction for the laws were put forward in a series of pamphlets which are listed in the Bibliography below

pressed by the representative assembly. Thirdly, few things are more surprising than the distance separating Fauchet's flights of oratory and the actual intentions which he made clear on his rare descents to earth. Although he stated that legislation should be submitted to primary assemblies, he always described the work of the latter as that of sanctioning the laws. He discussed this question on a high theoretical plane; the representatives wisely interpreted and the people joyfully accepted the precepts of natural law. In 1792 he was forced to make his position clear in relation to the King's trial. He objected to the use of the expression 'l'appel au peuple' because, he said, it conveyed a wrong impression. They were not proposing to appeal to the people on their representatives' decisions but only to obtain their sanction.[1] Thus it was not the people who were to make the ultimate decision; the role of the primary assemblies was to be in practice the purely formal one of the rubber stamp.

Thus, neither Gudin, nor Mercier, nor Fauchet, can strictly be said to have been in politics a disciple of Rousseau.[2] All three had already formed their political views before they began the study and exposition of the *Social Contract*. All three used Rousseau's authority to add weight to their personal views, although this involved considerable distortion of his theory. Where the *Social Contract* could not be used conveniently, it was examined, shown to be at fault and rejected. All three writers started from premises distinct from, and reached conclusions opposed to, those of Rousseau. At best they can be said to have taken the broad principles from the context of Rousseau's philosophy, and fitted them into their own, where they assumed an entirely different significance.

It is interesting to note that the blatant misinterpretation of Rousseau's theory by Mercier appeared to arouse no comment. Similarly, although Fauchet was satirized, there was no attack on his mishandling of the *Social Contract*. On the other hand, Gudin was criticized for his suggestion that Rousseau's theory, as it stood, was not applicable to eighteenth-century France, and for what was regarded as his presumption in supposing that

[1] *Opinion sur le jugement du ci-devant Roi*, 1792.

[2] For an opposite view on Fauchet, see Charrier, *Claude Fauchet*, etc., p. 158.

a supplement to the *Social Contract* was necessary at all.[1] Rousseau's name had become by 1791 so essential a part of the revolutionary religion, and so charged with patriotic emotions, that it was necessary that his theories should conform to those sentiments which the revolutionaries regarded as proper for the philosopher whom they had adopted as an idol and a prophet. Revolutionary readers preferred to be confirmed in their prejudices and their ignorance of Rousseau's political theory rather than enlightened as to the deep gulf which separated their own ambitions and assumptions from the views expressed in the *Social Contract.*

Only one writer appears to have found himself fully in agreement with the author of the *Social Contract.* This was a contributor to Prudhomme's journal *Révolutions de Paris* who wrote a series of articles from July 1789 onwards, attacking the representative system both at the national and at the local level. He is remarkable not only because he understood Rousseau's theory and used it with logical force to attack revolutionary practice, but also because as a rule the democrats were scornful of Rousseau's abstract approach to the problems arising out of the representative system. Unfortunately it is impossible to say with any certainty who he was. Hatin observed:

> Pour la *Révolutions de Paris* . . . on ne sait que vaguement quels furent ses rédacteurs; le nom dominant, c'est celui de Prudhomme, qui n'en était pourtant que l'éditeur, ou si l'on veut, le directeur-propriétaire.[2]

Silvain Maréchal, an admirer of Rousseau's works, was certainly a contributor to this journal, and it was he who initiated, through its pages, the establishment of a fund for the erection of a statue to Rousseau in 1790. By far the most able contributor, however, until his premature death, in September 1790, was Loustalot, and it is with his name that the views expressed in Prudhomme's journal are mainly associated, rather than

[1] *Mercure de France*, 12 Feb. 1791, p. 150. On the other hand the anti-revolutionary journal *Les Sabats Jacobites* approved Gudin's use of the *Social Contract* to strengthen the claims of the monarchy, but pointed out, 'Les œuvres de J. J. Rousseau ressemblent à l'arche sacrée à laquelle personne n'osait toucher. C'est du moins ce qu'on a cru jusqu'à présent'. See No. I, 1791. This journal lasted for only twenty-five numbers, none of which were dated.

[2] E. Hatin, *Bibliographie de la presse périodique*, etc., 1866, p. 148.

with that of Sylvain Maréchal. The latter indeed, according to Hatin, was a minor contributor until after Loustalot's death.[1]

These articles, in which Rousseau's authority was used to attack the representative system, were a particular feature of those editions of *Révolutions de Paris* published during 1789 and 1790. References to Rousseau were made in this context after September 1790, but by no means so frequently. Because of the coincidence of the change in tone with Loustalot's death, we may therefore tentatively conclude that Loustalot was their author.

The main accusation launched against the representative system in the pages of *Révolutions de Paris* was that a new aristocracy was being formed in the National Assembly and in the new local assemblies. This complaint was elaborated with constant reference to, and quotations from, the *Social Contract*; it was argued that Rousseau had shown sovereignty to be inalienable and the general will incapable of representation, and that the greatest possible participation in public affairs was necessary in order that the citizens might acquire those habits of virtue which he had regarded as the real constitution of the state. It was conceded that in a country of the size of France a representative system was advisable, but it should be regarded only as a necessary expedient and not as something good in itself. Rousseau had shown that the institution of representation was a derivation of feudalism, detrimental to the dignity of man, and had argued that for the safety of the citizens and the protection of liberty deputies should be empowered to act only within the limits of their instructions. The best way to ensure an active and watchful body of citizens, it was argued, was to encourage the greatest possible participation in public affairs, and since participation in national government presented inconveniences, it was in the smaller units of the municipalities that it could, at any rate as a beginning, be practically encouraged.

This process of education in citizenship was regarded as particularly necessary for France, because the French people had been so long excluded from public affairs. They had become so accustomed to following their own interests that the

[1] See also Robinet, *Dictionnaire de la Révolution*, etc., 1899, II, 455, 456.

virtues of citizenship were alien to them. It was necessary, therefore, that they should be drawn into public life by all possible channels, and primary assemblies provided the best means by which they could be taught to co-operate for the public welfare. The National Assembly was accused of going about its task of regeneration the wrong way round; Rousseau had warned his readers in the *Social Contract*, and in the *Considérations sur le gouvernement de Pologne*, that good laws could not be established, or if established could not be maintained, by a corrupt people. It was necessary to lay the foundations before building the superstructure, which could only be slowly erected on the basis of civic virtues. 'Sans les mœurs chacun se préfère à la patrie, les passions particulières conspirent contre la volonté générale et il ne peut exister d'esprit public.'[1]

While the main attack on the representative system was directed against the municipal assemblies and particularly against the Paris Commune, the whole theory of representation was at the same time condemned, and on Rousseau's authority it was denied that the National Assembly could claim to exercise sovereign powers on behalf of the nation. The identification, commonly made, between the will of the people and the will of their representatives, was rejected; the National Assembly was not France, it was argued, any more than the Commune was Paris. Alone among the revolutionary writers of this period this contributor to the *Révolutions de Paris* put his finger on the weak link in revolutionary logic. How could the deputy, simply by the fact of having been elected, be empowered to express the will of those who elected him? The power of expressing the general will could not be transmitted, and to will the election of certain deputies was quite distinct from willing the laws which these deputies would then make. If the expression of the general will was limited simply to the election of deputies, then a body of representatives with practically independent powers was created, and a particular will automatically formed. While, as Rousseau had seen, it was possible for a particular will to be in accordance with the general will at some points, such accord could not possibly be more than transitory and accidental.

[1] *Révolutions de Paris*, 31 October–7 November 1789, No. XVII, p. 2.

Écoutez donc citoyens, un politique qui est au-dessus de tous les éloges, et qui ne peut être soupçonné d'esprit de parti; la souveraineté ne peut être représentée, dit Jean-Jacques, elle consiste essentiellement dans la volonté générale, et la volonté générale ne se représente point.[1]

It was therefore advocated, in the pages of *Révolutions de Paris*, that the participation of the citizens should be secured not only at the local but also at the national level, by means both of the mandate, and the submission of all legislation in draft form to primary assemblies. This, it was admitted, presented much greater practical difficulty than the participation of the citizens in local government, but, as Rousseau had written: 'Où la liberté est tout, les inconvéniens ne sont rien.'[2]

Yet it must not be thought that even the author of these articles was making a purely disinterested exposition of Rousseau's theory. This journal, as its title suggests, dealt almost exclusively with events in the capital, and its arguments in favour of limiting the powers of representatives and training the citizens in public responsibility were directed against the Commune of Paris. They must be seen against the background of the actual struggle between the Commune and the sections, in which the *Révolutions de Paris* took an active interest. Nor was this journal alone in its attack on the Commune. There was a real fear that in the new local assemblies, whose members were frequently drawn from the ranks of the wealthy, a new privileged class was in process of being formed. The abbé Fauchet, himself a member of the Commune, constantly urged his fellow deputies to regard themselves as the 'mandataires' of the sections; the district of the Cordeliers, in September 1789, attempted to reduce its own delegates to the role of 'mandataires', binding them on oath to their instructions, and forbidding them to decide on any issue which had not been first referred back to their electors. Both Fauchet and the Cordeliers were supported by Prudhomme's journal.[3]

[1] Ibid. 14–21 November 1789, No. XX, p. 17.

[2] Ibid. 28 November–5 December 1789, No. XXI, p. 18.

[3] Ibid. 14, 21 November 1789, No. XIX, p. 24 ff. Fauchet represented the district of Saint Roche. For his views on representation see *La Religion Nationale* and the pamphlets in the Bibliography below.

Thus, while the author of these articles was obviously impressed by Rousseau's theories, he was also clearly concerned with their immediate usefulness in the political controversy in which the journal was engaged. Despite his concern with practical issues, however, he expounded Rousseau's theories with greater accuracy and integrity than any other revolutionary writer during the period 1789–91. The belief that in this journal we have an example—perhaps the only example—of a genuine attempt to apply the theories of the *Social Contract* to revolutionary politics is confirmed strikingly by the fact that hand in hand with the demand for a limitation of the powers of representatives went a demand for a stronger executive power. In September 1789, Bailly, then Mayor of Paris, was censured by the *Ami du Peuple* for having sought to usurp the municipal government. Bailly had complained in an address to the districts that the mayoral office had insufficient authority in the proposed organization of the municipalities, and that there should be a greater concentration of the executive power in a city of the size of Paris. His arguments were quoted at length in the *Révolutions de Paris*, and enthusiastically applauded. The controversy provided the occasion for a further exposition of the theories of the *Social Contract*. In perhaps no other source, either revolutionary or anti-revolutionary, can be found so clear an exposition of Rousseau's distinction between the sovereign and the Prince; that is, between the collective exercise of the power of legislation on the one hand, and the delegated function of administration on the other.[1]

The arguments put forward in this journal are, as far as my reading goes, unique. It is true that the writer used the *Social Contract* to add weight to arguments on a specific political problem about which he already clearly held strong views. Nevertheless, in the pages of the *Révolutions de Paris* Rousseau's authority was actually used in support of a practical policy which was reasonably consistent with his theoretical position. The writer had studied the *Social Contract* with care, and stated Rousseau's theories accurately and without distortion. It is hardly surprising that on occasions the journal should print

[1] Ibid. 26 September–3 October 1789, No. XII, p. 34 ff.

comments like the following on the claim that the Revolution was inspired by Rousseau:

Jean-Jacques Rousseau, le plus parfait et surtout le plus désintéressé des publicistes, passe pour être le père de notre constitution. Si notre constitution peut être considérée comme l'enfant de J. J. Rousseau, il faut du moins convenir que nos représentants l'ont furieusement estropié, et je doute que Rousseau, revenant au monde, demeurât d'accord de la paternité.[1]

[1] Ibid. 26 February–5 March 1791, No. 86, p. 378.

CHAPTER VII

The Revolutionary Theory of Sovereignty

REVOLUTIONARY speakers and writers frequently asserted, as Rousseau had in the *Social Contract*, that the laws were the expression of the general will. This principle was officially proclaimed in Article III of the Declaration of Rights. The constant use of the expression 'la volonté générale' has been regarded by many historians as evidence of the influence of the *Social Contract*. Indeed, the conclusion that Rousseau was the originator of the idea of the general will as used by the revolutionaries was made as early as 1789, as we have seen, by Isnard.[1]

Reasons for doubting that the revolutionaries were familiar with the theories put forward in the *Social Contract* have already been given, and it is not proposed to repeat these in relation to the revolutionary use of the phrase 'la volonté générale'. It seems fairly clear from the way in which the revolutionaries used the expression that they were not familiar with the Rousseauist interpretation. Moreover there is no reason to suppose that the *Social Contract* was the only source from which this expression could have been derived. Derathé,[2] and Léon,[3] have shown that while Rousseau gave to the idea a connotation which is peculiar to his own political thought, nevertheless the concept of the general will was not new when the *Social Contract* was written. Rousseau was neither the first nor the only political theorist to use the expression. Montesquieu, Holbach and

[1] Isnard, *Le Principe*, etc. See Ch. VI.

[2] R. Derathé, *Rousseau et la science politique de son temps*, 1950.

[3] P. L. Léon, 'L'idée de volonté générale chez J. J. Rousseau et ses antécedents historiques', *Archives de Philosophie du droit et de sociologie juridique* 1936, Nos, 3–4.

Diderot used it in works published prior to 1762.[1] It was also used by an Italian writer, J. V. Gravina, in a treatise on political theory.[2] Translated into French in 1766, this work ran into two editions and enjoyed considerable success.[3] The fact that the expression was used by the members of the Parlement of Rouen in 1771[4] suggests that by this date it already enjoyed a fairly wide currency. It seems unlikely that the *parlementaires* were students of the *Social Contract* or that they would knowingly utilize a phrase drawn from that work.

It is relevant to point out that in 1789 the expression 'the general will' was only one of many used by revolutionary speakers and writers to denote the idea of the interests of the nation as opposed to those of minorities. They also used the phrases 'la volonté nationale', 'le voeu commun', 'l'intérêt national', 'l'intérêt général', 'l'intérêt commun', 'la volonté commune' and so on. The use of such phrases is particularly well illustrated by Sieyès' famous pamphlet *Qu'est-ce que le Tiers État?* which repeats these phrases constantly, but refers only once to the general will. The expression gained a pre-eminent place in revolutionary lore and language, and it was given official recognition by its inclusion in the Declaration of Rights. This may have been because it was regarded as particularly appropriate. It is also probable that the previous use of the expression by political philosophers had endowed it with special weight. As interest in Rousseau's name as a revolutionary symbol gained strength, the expression no doubt received added recommendation because of Rousseau's use of it. There is no evidence, however, that the revolutionaries derived either the phrase itself or their understanding of it from the *Social Contract*.

[1] See Diderot's article 'Cité' in *Encyclopédie*, III; also the article 'Droit Naturel', ibid. v. reprinted Vaughan, I, 423. Whether or not Rousseau was influenced by Diderot's concept of the general will is discussed by Vaughan, I, 425. Hendel takes the view that it was Rousseau who called the attention of Diderot to the idea of the general will in the works of Pufendorf. See *J. J. Rousseau, Moralist*, 1934, I, 100. The expression was also used by Holbach in his *Système Social*, II, 21, and by Montesquieu in the *Esprit des Lois*, VII, chs. i–vii.

[2] J. V. Gravina, *Opera seu originum Juris Civilis libri tres*, Venice, 1739, translated into French in 1776 under the title, *L'Esprit de lois romaines*. Montesquieu referred to this work and quoted from it. See *Esprit des Lois*, I, ch. iii, pp. 11, 12.

[3] C. Hendel, *J. J. Rousseau, Moralist*, I, 99, 100, 102.

[4] *Remontrances du Parlement de Rouen*, 1771. See R. Bickart, *Les Parlements et la notion de souveraineté nationale au xviiie siècle*, 1932.

Dr. Eric Thompson states that although the revolutionaries constantly referred to the general will, they used the phrase vaguely, and never actually explained what they meant by it.[1] This, however, is not the case: revolutionary speakers and writers frequently defined the general will. They equated it with the will of the majority. The general will, wrote Sieyès, is formed by the will of the majority.[2] For the people to be free, stated M. de Sèze, they must obey the general will, which always resides in the majority.[3] The will of the greatest number, asserted one pamphleteer, alone forms the general will.[4] The victorious advance of the general will, wrote another, demonstrates the immense majority which supports the Revolution.[5] Yet another proposed that no measure should be accepted unless the majority in support of it was large enough to ensure that the general will was being expressed. He applauded the proposal made by La Cretelle, and supported by other deputies, that a two-thirds majority would be 'assez nombreuse pour qu'on soit assuré de l'invariabilité de la volonté générale'.[6]

The general will was described not only as the majority will but also as the sum of particular wills. Discussing the formulation of the general will, M. de Sèze asserted:

Si la nation faisait elle-même les loix, elle les ferait conformer à l'intérêt général, parce que du concours de tous les intérêts particuliers se forme l'intérêt public.[7]

Pétion de Villeneuve stated:

Si chacun pouvait faire entendre sa volonté particulière, la réunion de toutes ces volontés formerait véritablement la volonté générale; ce serait le dernier degré de perfection politique.[8]

[1] Eric Thompson, *Popular sovereignty and the French Constituent Assembly*, 1952. p. 35.

[2] Sieyès, *Préliminaire de la Constitution*, 1789, p. 22.

[3] Sèze, *Opinion sur la sanction royale*, 1789, p. 8.

[4] Anon., *Motion d'un campagnard*, etc., 1789, p. 3.

[5] *Adresse de la Société des Amis de la Constitution aux sociétés qui lui sont affiliées*, 1791, p. 8.

[6] Anon., *Examen impartiel* etc., 1789, p. 3.

[7] Sèze, *Opinion sur la sanction royale*, 1789, p. 4.

[8] Pétion de Villeneuve, *Opinion sur l'appel au peuple*, 1789, p. 5.

The authors of a Jacobin pamphlet described the general will as the expression of all wills and the result of all interests.[1] A writer in the *Bouche de Fer* referred to 'la volonté générale qui n'est que le résultat des volontés partielles de tous les individus'.[2] A speaker in the National Assembly stated the principle:

Que la volonté du plus grand nombre étant la loi de tous, chaque citoyen a le droit de concourir à la formation des loix en exprimant son voeu particulier.[3]

The same arguments were used by those writers who advocated the system of mandates or the 'appel au peuple'. They argued that the general will could be computed more clearly if heads were counted over the whole citizen community instead of simply counting them in the National Assembly. François Robert advocated both the mandate and the 'appel au peuple' for this reason. The general will could most accurately be calculated, he argued, by assessing the majority feeling in the *cahiers*, and by counting the votes in local assemblies.[4] The same arguments were used by Fauchet[5] and Pétion de Villeneuve.[6]

When an examination is made of the reasons why the revolutionaries thought that the will of the majority was the proper basis for the law, it is possible to discern some similarities between the arguments which they used and the assumptions made in the *Social Contract*. These similarities, however, are superficial. They arise from the fact that the revolutionaries were concerned with exactly the same major social and political problems as had interested Rousseau. They wished, that is, to establish equality under the law, to destroy privilege, and to guard against its re-emergence. Like Rousseau, though in rather a different sense, they accepted the theory of the sovereignty of the people as the means of guaranteeing liberty and the equality of rights. The practical conclusions to which the

[1] *Adresse de la société des Amis de la Constitution*, etc., 1791, p. 3.
[2] *Bouche de Fer*, 27 January 1791, No. 11, p. 173.
[3] *Journal des Débats*, 1 August 1789.
[4] Robert, *Le républicanisme*, etc., 1790.
[5] *Bouche de Fer*, November 1790, No. 15, p. 236; December 1790, No. 31, pp. 481–500.
[6] *Opinion sur l'appel au peuple*, etc., 1789.

revolutionaries came, however, were fundamentally different from the conclusions reached by Rousseau.

The revolutionaries perceived, as Rousseau had done, that when the laws were made by a privileged minority, they were directed towards the interests of that minority. They therefore concluded that the power of making the laws ought to be vested in the majority. In *Qu'est-ce que le Tiers État?* Sieyès argued that the laws should express the will and serve the interests of the Third Estate because the Third Estate contained the numerical preponderance of the citizens. Preponderance of numbers was emphasized as the best guarantee that the laws would be directed toward general, rather than particular, ends.

If the law was to be general in its ends, it had also to be general in its origins. It was impossible for the law to be equal for all if some of those who participated in making it enjoyed privileges under it. The creation of any privileged corporation, Sieyès argued, gave rise to an *imperium in imperio*, for a privileged corporation would always put its own interests before those of the whole people. Thus it was necessary that the individual should be reduced, in Sieyès' words, 'to the numerical one'.[1] It was in this sense that the revolutionaries argued that the general will was the sum of particular wills. On the other hand they used the expression 'la volonté particulière' in two ways. Sometimes they spoke of it as being in opposition to the general will, and sometimes as the component part of the general will. The difference between these two usages depended upon whether the will in question belonged to a corporation or an individual citizen. The latter was admissible as a part of the general will; the former was not.

There was no suggestion, in these arguments, that the citizen should appeal to any transcendental standard of justice, or that he should consult his own conscience. The formulation of the general will did not involve the weighing of ethical values but rather the assessment of individual interests. If each individual citizen voted according to his own independent interests, then it was assumed that by mathematical law the interests of the majority of citizens would predominate. In fact, of course, the main body of the citizens was never called upon to participate

[1] Sieyès, *Sur la question du véto royal*, 1789, p. 6.

in legislation. The actual formulation of the laws, which in Rousseau's view was synonymous with the expression of the general will, was regarded by the revolutionaries as the function of the elected deputies of the people. Thus the citizens were excluded from participating in the expression of the general will in the sense in which Rousseau understood the phrase; their function was simply that of voting at elections.

At the same time, however, the will of the majority was equated with justice in so far as it was regarded as the main guarantee of individual rights. It had been the minorities which had perpetuated unnatural privileges and inequalities. The will of the majority on the contrary ensured equality of rights. Thus some writers regarded the will of the majority as expressing the precepts of natural law, and claimed that it was only through the majority will that the canons of natural law could be discovered. Daunou claimed: 'L'existence d'une loi naturelle ne peut être manifestée que par l'assentiment du plus grand nombre, et l'intérêt collectif ne peut être declaré que par la majeure partie des individus.'[1] Fauchet expressed the same view, in a more elaborate form. The will of the people expressed in a majority vote, he asserted, was the one infallible source of just laws in the state. Men were essentially good, and were able to understand natural law by their reason and by the teaching of religion. The Revolution had clarified the people's reason and enlightened them as to their true interests. Whatever the majority willed was henceforward in accordance with natural law. Thus the validity of the law was ultimately judged by the criterion of the numbers who supported it, and the possibility that the majority might on some occasions be mistaken was ruled out.[2]

Not all writers, however, felt it necessary to idealize the concept of the majority will by associating it with the canons of natural law. Some of them stated quite baldly that the will of the majority needed no justification; a law was valid because the majority had willed it, even if it could be shown to be unjust. Servan wrote that only the nation had the right to establish a constitution, and even if the constitution were

[1] Daunou, *Le Contrat Social des Français*, 1789, p. 6.
[2] *Bouche de Fer*, No. 7. 17 January 1791. p. 107.

thoroughly vicious, it would still be legitimate. On the other hand, a constitution established by a despot, even if it were just, remained invalid.[1] Sieyès expressed the same view. Although he had supported his arguments in *Qu'est-ce que le Tiers État?* by asserting that the Third Estate contained within itself all the useful and constructive elements in society, he did not regard this as the main reason why the Third Estate should make the laws. Ultimately, the claims of the Third Estate were based on their numerical superiority. In a speech which he made in the National Assembly, opposing the royal veto, Sieyès asserted that the minority must always submit to the majority, even if it were the case, as the constitutional monarchists argued, that the minority were the more enlightened.[2] Basire, speaking in the Jacobin Club, was later to make a complete reversal of Rousseau's principle. It was not enough, he said, for the law to be judged good; it must also be shown to be general.[3]

In the last resort this came down to the denial that there was, in fact, any standard of justice other than that which the nation itself created. A writer denying the existence of 'natural' equality, could argue that all rights existed solely because the nation willed them and the public force maintained them.[4] Sieyès himself held that a law was valid simply because the nation, or the majority of the nation, had willed it, and no appeal to standards of universal justice was possible or relevant. The nation itself was the only criterion of justice.

La Nation existe avant tout, elle est l'origine de tout, sa volonté est toujours légale, elle est la loi elle-même.[5]

Again,

La Nation est tout ce qu'elle peut être, par cela seul qu'elle est. . . . La volonté nationale . . . n'a besoin que de sa réalité pour être toujours légale; elle est l'origine de toute légalité.[6]

[1] Servan, *Essai sur la formation des assemblées*, etc., 1789, p. 12. Compare Mercier, *J. J. Rousseau*, etc., 1791, I, ii, 109.

[2] Sieyès, *Sur la question du véto royal*, 1789, pp. 14–15.

[3] Quoted by Champion, *Rousseau et la Révolution française*, ch. xviii, pp. 235–6, n.

[4] *Bouche de Fer*, December 1790, No. 27, Rassron de Trouillet, 'Mémoire sur les vraies bases de l'association', p. 425.

[5] Sieyès, *Qu'est-ce que le Tiers État?*, 1789, ed. Champion, p. 67.

[6] Ibid. p. 68.

It should be plain by now that the revolutionaries defined the general will in terms which were quite different from those used by Rousseau. They do not appear to have been conscious of Rousseau's definition; they did not discuss it. The expression was a useful one to christen an idea of law born out of their experience and requiring no justification. The importance of majority rule and the minority was the distinction between the nation and the parasitic aristocracy, between equality of rights and unjust privileges. The minority were the enemies, first of the nation and then of the Revolution. 'Les nobles et les prêtres, messieurs' asserted one speaker, and he spoke for the revolutionaries as a whole, 'Voilà les ennemis'.[1] Thus, when the revolutionaries talked and wrote about the general will they meant a will which was in conformity with the interests of the nation as apart from the interests of the privileged orders and corporations. They were in agreement with Rousseau's theory, and also with that of the Ancien Régime, that there must be a single will ruling the nation. The revolutionary interpretation of this was that any individual who deviated from the generally accepted view must inevitably be an aristocrat, and risked being classed as an enemy of the nation and the Revolution. These assumptions were confirmed by the recalcitrant attitude of the noblesse in the early stages of the Revolution, and later by the emigration and the threat of counter-revolution. The subsequent revolutionary manifestations of collectivism, dictatorship and intolerance were the products of the revolutionary situation itself, and can be explained in terms of practical politics. The revolutionaries had no need to look for them in the pages of the *Social Contract*, nor is there any evidence that they did so.[2]

From Rousseau's concept of the general will was derived his refusal to accept representation. Here again the ideas of 1789 differed in fundamental respects from those put forward in the *Social Contract*. In particular Rousseau had insisted that the general will was incapable of being represented, and that sove-

[1] J. C. Simonne, 'Discours sur la loi à faire contre les émigrations,' *Société des Amis de la Constitution*, etc., 25 December 1791, p. 9.

[2] See Jean Belin, *La logique d'une idée-force; l'idée d'utilité sociale et la Révolution française, 1789–92*, 1939.

reignty, which consisted essentially in the expression of the general will, was indivisible. The pamphleteers and orators of 1789 constantly referred to the sovereignty of the people as inalienable and indivisible, but they did not interpret these words as Rousseau had done. They distinguished between sovereignty and sovereign rights. The former was vested inalienably in the people, as the ultimate source of all political power; the latter could be delegated to representatives, and indeed had to be so in a country of the size of France, since otherwise they could not be exercised at all. Moreover, this delegation was final. Once the deputies had been elected, they and they alone were capable of expressing the general will. The will of the king, or of any private individual, or any assembly of individuals other than the National Assembly, was regarded as a particular or partial will. Thus when the revolutionaries spoke of the inalienable and indivisible character of sovereignty, they meant that the sovereign rights of the nation were vested indivisibly and inalienably in the representatives of the nation during the period for which they were elected. The general will was therefore expressed differently at two different levels. For the ordinary citizen, the expression of the general will meant the casting of a vote; for the elected deputy it meant the power of legislation.

This view was clearly contrary to Rousseau's principle that legislation was an act of sovereignty, incapable of being delegated. The revolutionaries asserted precisely the opposite principle that sovereign rights could not be exercised except by representatives. They did not, however, regard representation as involving any alienation of sovereignty, for they insisted that the will expressed by the representative assembly was the will of the people. Thus Robespierre asserted that every man had a right to govern himself and his own actions, a right which he carried with him into society. In a large society, however, this right could only be exercised by representatives. The will of the representatives had therefore to be respected as the will of the nation.[1] Sieyès similarly denied that any distinction could be made between the will of the people and that of their deputies. This, he said, was a most dangerous suggestion. It was obvious

[1] *Dire de M. de Robespierre . . . contre le véto royal*, etc., 1789. See *Discours*, VI, 86.

that five or six million citizens scattered over twenty-five thousand square miles could not possibly assemble to make the laws. Their only means of making their will known was to elect deputies, and once that had been done they renounced all claims to make the law themselves.[1]

The revolutionaries departed completely from the view which Rousseau had expressed both in the *Social Contract* and in the *Considérations sur le gouvernement de Pologne*, that the people's deputies could only be their stewards, bound by the instructions of their electors and incapable of willing in their name. This concept they identified with the preservation of aristocratic and local privilege. Revolutionary writers and speakers continued to use the word *mandat* and to describe the National Assembly as holding 'a mandate from the nation', but they completely transformed the idea of the mandate as it had been used by the aristocrats. Target, writing early in 1789, explained that the Estates General were being convened in order that the general will might be known. There was no single man, commune or *bailliage*, he wrote, which was not subject to that will. He therefore warned the electors that they should not try to tie their deputies down, by means of their *cahiers*, to local interests, but should encourage them to think and to act for France. They should give their deputies general guiding principles only:

> Instruisez, donnez vos mémoires . . . et non vos cahiers mesquins et limitatifs, exprimez vos vœux, enrichez nos répresentants de vos idées que les droits nationaux, les grands principes de la liberté publique et individuelle, respirent dans vos instructions.[2]

Similarly, Talleyrand, in his speech opposing the imperative mandate, argued that the general will could not be expressed by any local assembly, but could emerge only as a result of deliberation among the elected deputies of the whole nation, who must be free to come to a decision according to their consciences.[3] Robespierre argued in the same way. Only the nation, he asserted, was superior to the representative assembly,

[1] Sieyès, *Sur la question du véto royal*, 1789, p. 15.

[2] Target, *Les États Généraux*, etc., 1789, pp. 54–5.

[3] Talleyrand, *Discours . . . sur les mandats impératifs*, 1789.

and assuming that the nation could assemble, there and there alone would be found the proper judge of the work of the National Assembly. In fact, however, as Robespierre acknowledged, the nation never could assemble, and he denied that any part of the nation, in the form of a local assembly, could oppose its judgement to that of the elected deputies.[1] Against the claims of the Estates of Cambrésis he asserted that the only true representatives of the people of Cambrésis were the members of the National Assembly.[2]

The result was that, as Mounier was later to point out, the revolutionaries attributed to their representatives all those powers which Rousseau had regarded as being the inalienable property of the people.[3]

Can it be maintained that this view of representation originated in a misunderstanding of the *Social Contract*? Some writers and speakers quoted Rousseau's name and referred to the *Social Contract* in the arguments they put forward about popular sovereignty and representation. An analysis of such references does not, however, lead to the conclusion that the revolutionaries owed their views to the study of Rousseau. In the first place, these references are, on the whole, rare. I have found only one appeal to Rousseau's authority within the context of an argument about representation in the year 1788, and the writer was a conservative, who argued, on Rousseau's authority, that since sovereignty could not be represented, the only role which the deputies could hope to fill was that of 'intermédiaires' between prince and people.[4]

In general, Rousseau's name was used to support arguments which were already currently accepted. For example, in July 1789, Aubert de Vitry published anonymously a pamphlet entitled *Jean-Jacques Rousseau à l'Assemblée Nationale*. In this he used Rousseau's authority, quite unfairly of course, against any

[1] Robespierre, *Sur l'inviolabilité des députés*, 1789. *Discours*, VI, 429.

[2] On 9 November 1789, the Estates of Cambrésis formally disavowed all that their representatives had done in the National Assembly, and declared that the powers of their representatives were henceforward revoked. The Assembly accepted a motion proposed by Barnave, declaring the action of the Estates of Cambrésis null. See *Discours*, VI, 143, for Robespierre's argument.

[3] Mounier, *On the influence attributed to philosophers*, etc., p. 190.

[4] Anon., *Le disciple de Montesquieu*, etc., 1788, p. 94.

suggestion that the powers of the deputies should be limited, arguing that the people had delegated sovereign rights to their deputies, and that the latter had therefore full and final responsibility for drawing up a constitution. At the same time Vitry was perfectly aware that Rousseau's theories were in direct opposition to his own views. In a footnote he admitted that Rousseau had condemned representation,[1] but he added that whatever Rousseau had said, the fact remained that representation was the greatest political invention of modern times, and, in spite of this patent contradiction, he continued to use Rousseau's name.

The opportunist use of Rousseau's name to support popular revolutionary theory is illustrated by Théophile Mandar. In 1790 Mandar translated into French the work of the seventeenth-century English political writer Marchemont Needham, who, in 1656, had published a treatise on the sovereignty of the people. Needham's argument was that only a representative assembly could be trusted to exercise sovereign rights and to protect the people from tyranny. Théophile Mandar added to this work quotations drawn from the *Social Contract* and the *Considérations sur le gouvernement de Pologne*, selected to give the impression of complete accord between the theory of Rousseau and that of Needham. He also drew quotations from the works of Mably, Bossuet, Condillac, Montesquieu, Letrosne, Raynal and others, including nothing to suggest to anyone not familiar with these writers that their views differed, either from one another's or from those of Needham.[2]

The same inexactitude, if not deliberate misconstruction, was demonstrated by Laclos. Opposing the monarchists' claim that the king's person was inviolable, he asserted: 'Jean-Jacques Rousseau nous a dit dans son Contrat Social qu'en présence de l'Assemblée du peuple le prince n'existait point.'[3]

By the 'Assembly of the people', of course, he meant the assembly of their representatives, which was to distort completely Rousseau's theory.

[1] Aubert de Vitry, *Jean-Jacques Rousseau à l'Assemblée Nationale*, 1789, p. 44. This pamphlet was directed against the arguments put forward by Brissot, *Plan de conduite*, etc., and by Sieyès, *Préliminaire de la Constitution.*

[2] Théophile Mandar, *De la souveraineté du peuple*, etc., 1790.

[3] *Journal des Jacobins,* 18 July 1791, No. 25.

It is true that in some pamphlets in which the subject of representation was discussed Rousseau's name was mentioned, but this was by no means as frequently as has been assumed; and it was used so arbitrarily, and in relation to so many and such varied arguments, that it is impossible to regard the appeal to Rousseau as having particular significance in relation to the revolutionary theory of representation. In any case, the revolutionaries did not need to appeal to any particular philosopher for guidance in formulating their theory of representation. Indeed, those who revealed familiarity with the theories of the *Social Contract* were in the main critical of what they regarded as Rousseau's unrealistic attitude towards the representative system.

When the Estates General met in 1789 two views about the functions of representative assemblies already existed. One was the traditional view that the deputies were delegates, holding mandates from the orders and localities which had elected them; the contrary view was that which had been developed during the past fifty years by the Parlements. The first of these has already been mentioned in relation to d'Antraigues' *Mémoire*.[1] It was put forward in pamphlets during 1788–89 by members of the noblesse as well as by some members of the Third Estate. According to this view the deputy was bound by oath to the instructions contained in his *cahier* and was powerless to go outside these. The aristocratic and conservative exponents of this view based their case on precedent, referring to the traditions of past Estates General. D'Antraigues alone introduced abstract political principles to justify the mandate, appealing to the inalienable sovereignty of the people. At no point, however, in the controversy over the mandate during June and July 1789, was an appeal made to the authority of Rousseau by members of the first and second orders, to justify their determination to maintain the mandate.[2] Moreover, although in 1788 d'Antraigues had appealed to the principle of the sovereignty of the people, in 1789, as a member of the deputation of the noblesse appointed to discuss procedure with delegates from the

[1] See Ch. VI.

[2] The debates on the mandate were collected together in the *Mon. Réimp.*, Nos. 11, 12, 13 and 15, covering the period 24 June–8 July 1789. The material was mainly drawn from the *Journal des Débats* and from discourses published in pamphlet form.

Third Estate, he confined himself to precedent.[1] By the end of 1790 and by 1791, some aristocratic writers had learned enough of the language of the Revolution to be able to describe the position they had taken in the summer of 1789 as one of defending the people's sovereignty. In so doing a few of them pointed out that in adhering to the theory of the mandate, they had been acting as faithful disciples of Rousseau.[2] During May–July 1789, however, when the battle over the mandate was actually being fought, no references were made to the *Social Contract* in its defence.

The mandate was obviously unacceptable to the Third Estate. If in theory, as expounded in d'Antraigues' *Mémoire*, it was the logical conclusion to the acceptance of the principle of inalienable national sovereignty, in practice it was the means of perpetuating separate representation of the three orders, and of conserving privilege. The theory of the mandate was fundamentally conservative. D'Antraigues had put forward the mandate as the great constitutional bulwark of the French people, by which a united nation could defend its rights against the encroachments of despotism. It was, however, clear to the Third Estate that it was in fact also the bulwark of the noblesse against the encroachments of the Third Estate. D'Antraigues' *Mémoire* was indeed something of a red herring, for it called upon the nation to defend a constitution which, it might be argued, had never existed, against a despotism which had ceased to exist. As one critic pointed out, it was illogical on the part of d'Antraigues to defend the conservative principle of the mandate 'dans un ordre de choses tel que le peuple ne s'assemble que pour le changer'.[3]

There is no doubt that the revolutionaries were stimulated by the controversy over the mandate to formulate an alternative statement of the powers of representatives. The pamphlet literature of 1788–9 clearly reveals, however, that there already existed a fairly consistent and widely current view of representation upon which to build. This view owed nothing to the traditions of the Estates General, and very little to the abstract

[1] References to d'Antraigues' speeches are given in the Bibliography below.

[2] See Ch. X.

[3] Anon., *Lettres à quelques propriétaires*, etc., 1789, p. 5.

dogma of political theory. It was a restatement of arguments which had become familiar as a result of the struggles between the monarchy and the Parlements during the course of at least half a century. A study of the pamphlet literature of 1788–9 shows that the pamphleteers followed very closely the pattern of the Remonstrances of the Parlements, which had constantly asserted, in order to justify the claim to participate in legislation, that the people was sovereign. The Parlements argued that popular sovereignty had been an historic fact, both in the republics of classical antiquity and in the early history of the French nation. The primitive monarchy, they stated, had originated in a free contract between king and people, and under the first two dynasties the entire male adult population had assembled on the Champ de Mars annually to exercise their sovereign rights by directly participating in legislation. The growth of the population had made it necessary to delegate the exercise of sovereign rights to representatives. In the absence of the Estates General the Parlements claimed that it was their duty to represent the nation. Their main task they regarded as the preservation of the ancient constitution. This, they asserted, comprised certain fundamental laws by which the king was bound and which he had no power to change. These fundamental laws were the expression of the people's sovereignty, originating in the primitive contract, enshrined in custom and at all times reflecting the people's will. In the words of the author of the Remonstrance of the Parlement of Rouen, in 1771, these laws 'furent de tout temps l'expression de la volonté générale'.[1]

The expression of such views was not confined to private addresses to the king. On the contrary, the Parlements took every opportunity to bring their grievances to the notice of the public, and to enlist the support of public opinion. Professor Cobban wrote of the Parlements:

Steadily, throughout the century they had appealed to the people against royal authority. The 'remonstrances', which were supposed

[1] Quoted by Roger Bickart. See p. 88, n. 4 above. For the Remonstrances of the eighteenth century see also: Jules Flammeront, *Remontrances du Parlement de Paris au XVIIIe siècle*, 1888–93, III, 1768–88; and André Lemaire, *Les lois fondamentales de la monarchie française*, 1907.

to be addressed privately to the king, they had turned into public manifestoes, and circulated widely. Of the Grand Remonstrances of 1758, more than 20,000 copies had been sold within a few weeks. The 'remonstrances' were often written in highly emotional language for the purpose of inflaming opinion, and Mathiez is surely right in attributing to them a far greater influence in spreading disrespect for the monarchy and the established form of government than was exercised by the writings of the philosophers, who were for the most part far from anti-monarchical.[1]

The views of the Parlements were given further publicity in secretly circulated pamphlets.[2] Immediately before the Revolution the Parlements were more than ever in the public eye, and more than ever appealed to the people for support in their struggle with royal authority. Their last and fatal triumph was in 1788 when they 'came back on the crest of a great wave of public feeling'.[3]

A theory of representation based on the sovereignty of the people was therefore already in existence prior to the convening of the Estates General. The concept of a representative assembly acting on behalf of the sovereign nation had already been evolved by the Parlements. Nor were the theories of Rousseau necessary to persuade the deputies of the National Assembly that they were competent to alter the fundamental laws of the state, and re-frame the social compact. This position could be reached by a simple, logical deduction from the arguments which the *parlementaires* had used. The latter had regarded themselves as 'intermédiaires'; their role was to protect the fundamental constitution. Nevertheless they had justified their claim to participate in legislation by asserting the sovereignty of the people. They had claimed that this participation was

[1] A. Cobban, 'The Parlements of France in the eighteenth century', *History*, xxx (1950), p. 79. Mme. Roland wrote that she took an immense interest in the conflicts between the court and the Parlements, and that she procured all the Remonstrances she could. She was most pleased, she said, by those which were most boldly expressed. See *Vie Privée*, I, 109.

[2] Felix Rocquain, *L'Esprit révolutionnaire avant la Révolution*, 1878. This writer gives a list of the pamphlets and brochures circulated between 1774 and 1776 in which it was argued: that the King held his power from the nation, and not from God; that the power of the King was limited; that revolt against despotism was an act of virtue. See ch. vii, p. 32; ch. viii, pp. 99, 123 and ch. ix, pp. 149, 150.

[3] Cobban, loc. cit., p. 79.

necessary in order to ensure that the royal government acted in conformity with the fundamental laws of the state. They asserted that only the nation was capable of changing these, and that in acting as their guardians they were expressing the will of the people. It is true that the idea of an ancient constitution was seized on by conservative writers in an attempt to forestall the revolutionaries. Nevertheless, the ideas of an original compact and of a fundamental constitution have obvious revolutionary significance. Once it had been accepted that such a constitution existed, and once this concept had been joined to the idea of the sovereignty of the people, it was not difficult to take the further step and to conclude that the nation could reassert its historic rights and restate its fundamental laws. The Parlements, by claiming to act in the name of the nation and to express its will, had pointed the way to the sovereignty of the revolutionary assemblies.

The revolutionaries parted company with the Parlements over their claim that the deputies of the National Assembly should not simply participate in legislation, but should lay down new fundamental laws, and their insistence that the will of the nation could be expressed only by its elected representatives. This extreme statement of the powers of representatives was not, however, a ready-made doctrine drawn from political theory. It was rather the fruit of practical experience, matured under the pressure of political strife. If the revolutionaries had had at their disposal a ready made theory of a popular sovereign assembly, it is difficult to see why they did not assert it earlier, at least as soon as the decision to convene the Estates General was made. In fact, the majority of the pamphleteers of 1788 and the first half of 1789 fall into two main categories: either they discuss past Estates General, searching for precedents, or else they repeat the general arguments about sovereignty, the growth of population and the need for representation, which the Parlements had made familiar. The revolutionary theory of representation was crystallized during the course of the practical struggle by which the Estates General became the National Assembly. The revolutionaries were obliged first to formulate their views in answer to the logic of the imperative mandate, and secondly to justify their claim to frame a new and binding constitution for France. The revolutionary theory of representation evolved in reply to a series of specific challenges, rather than from the pre-revolutionary study of the *Social Contract*, or indeed of any abstract work of political philosophy.

CHAPTER VIII

The Critics of the Social Contract

It is important to emphasize that between 1789 and 1791 the main critics of the *Social Contract* were drawn not from the ranks of the opponents of the Revolution but from those of the revolutionaries themselves. Only one serious attack on Rousseau's political theory from an anti-revolutionary source has been discovered. This was the pamphlet by Isnard, to which reference has already been made. The detailed criticism of Rousseau came from those who, at any rate up to the time when they were writing, agreed with and supported the achievements of the Revolution, or who, if they were writing during 1788 or the early months of 1789, put forward views about representation and sovereignty which were later adopted by the National Assembly.

Reference has already been made to the view of Professor Talmon that the chief exponent of Rousseauism in 1789 was the abbé Sieyès.[1] In fact, Sieyès differed from Rousseau in respect of the three principles which are crucial to the latter's political thought: law, the general will and representation. In Sieyès' view, law was simply what the nation willed; the general will was the sum of individual wills, and the ordinary citizen's share in the expression of the general will was limited to the exercise of the vote. Once the representative assembly had been elected, the citizen was obliged to accept the assembly's decisions as law. Sieyès admitted only one situation in which the will of the elected deputies of the people might be subject to modification. In July 1789, he put forward the view that the work of a constituent assembly ought to be subject to the scrutiny and

[1] Talmon, *Origins*, etc., pp. 69–75. See Ch. II.

sanction of a convention elected for that specific purpose, before it could be regarded as valid. Once the constitution was established, the representatives became the exclusive agents of sovereignty, and until that time, no other assembly or corporation could question or set itself up against those who had been elected by the people for the purpose of drawing up a new constitution.[1]

There is no reason to suppose that these views were based on a misinterpretation of the *Social Contract*. In the *Notice sur la vie de Sieyès*, which was published in 1796 and which Sieyes personally approved before publication, Condillac, Locke and Mably were listed as his favourite authors.[2] Van Deusen, in his study of Sieyès' political thought, insisted that there is no work by Sieyès, still extant, in which Rousseau's name is mentioned.[3] On one occasion, however, Sieyès did express an opinion on Rousseau's political theory. It was preserved in an essay by a writer who had access to manuscript notes which are no longer in existence. From this account it would appear that Sieyès regarded Rousseau's contribution to political theory as rudimentary. He wrote:

> Rousseau. Ils prennent les commencements de la société pour les principes de l'art social, dont les Français n'avaient pas l'idée il y a peu d'années, et dont le nom a été hasardé pour la première fois dans les 'Moyens d'exécution'. Que diraient-ils si l'on entreprenait la construction d'un vaisseau de ligne avec la seule théorie employée par les sauvages dans la construction de leurs radeaux? Tous les arts se perdraient en reculant ainsi à leur origine. L'art en toutes choses est venu fort tard. Il suppose de grands progrès depuis leur premier âge.

Of Rousseau himself Sieyès wrote that he was 'un philosophe aussi parfait de sentiment que faible de vue'.[4]

[1] Sieyès, *Préliminaire de la constitution,* 1789. Talmon attributes the contrary view to him.

[2] C. E. Oelsner, *Notice sur la vie de Sieyès*, 1796, p. 49.

[3] G. Van Duesen, *Sieyès, his life and nationalism*, 1933.

[4] C. A. Sainte-Beuve, *Causeries du Lundi*, 'Étude sur Sieyès', by Edmonde de Beauverger, 1851, p. 155. For an account of Sieyès' political thought in relation to that of Rousseau see also P. Bastid, *Sieyès et sa pensée*, 1939, particularly pp. 308, 309, 567, Y. Koung, *Théorie constitutionelle de Sieyès*, 1934, and A. Mathiez, 'La Révolution française et la théorie de la dictature', *Revue Historique*, 1929, pp. 304–15.

Criticism of Rousseau's theories was made by writers of very different viewpoints. They were all agreed, however, that his political thought was too abstract to be of practical value to revolutionary France, and that representation was a necessary and a salutary institution. These arguments were used by two anonymous pamphleteers writing early in 1789. The author of *Théorie des États Généraux ou la France régénérée* was an Anglophile, whom one might expect to be hostile to Rousseau. The author of the pamphlet *De l'autorité de Montesquieu dans la Révolution présente* was, as his title suggests, an admirer of Montesquieu, whose theory he compared to that of Rousseau, to the latter's disadvantage. Also in 1789, Mme. de Staël published the *Lettres sur les ouvrages et le caractère de J. J. Rousseau*, and Servan his *Essai sur la forme des assemblées nationales, provinciales et municipales en France*. Both criticized Rousseau for his unrealistic attitude towards the representative system. In 1790 Gudin criticized Rousseau in his *Supplément au Contrat Social* for his idealistic preoccupation with small states and for his failure to relate the question of the expression of the general will to the needs of great nations. In the following year, Mercier,[1] while distorting Rousseau's theory of representation, nevertheless took exception to his principle that the people should ratify the laws. An anonymous contributor to the *Mercure de France* argued that Rousseau was entirely wrong in maintaining that sovereign rights could not be delegated.[2]

It might have been expected that criticisms of Rousseau's theories should have come from Anglophiles and from constitutional monarchists, but not that they should also have aroused the hostility of democrats and republicans. Yet Fauchet, Brissot and François Robert were all critical of Rousseau, although they put forward proposals for the closer supervision of representatives. Brissot had suggested as early as 1789 that the constitution should be submitted to primary assemblies.[3] In 1791 he proposed that the work of the Assembly should be submitted for ratification by a popular convention.[4] Fauchet,

[1] Mercier, *J. J. Rousseau*, etc., 1791.

[2] 'Observations sur l'ouvrage de M. de Calonne', etc., *Mercure de France*. See 9 April 1791, p. 84 ff, and 30 April, p. 180 ff.

[3] Brissot, *Plan de Conduite*, etc., 1789.

[4] Brissot, *Discours sur les conventions*, etc., 1791.

as a member of the Paris Commune, was in the van of the attack on the new aristocracy created by the representative system.[1] In spite of this they both criticized Rousseau's rejection of the representative system. Robert, an extreme democrat and republican, even accused him of having been an enemy of liberty because he had denied that direct democracy and republicanism were applicable in large states.[2]

Despite the fact that some advocated the virtual independence, and others the closer supervision of deputies, the arguments which they used to attack Rousseau were similar. They questioned his description of the ideal small state in which men exercised sovereignty directly, and asked whether, in fact, men did not enjoy greater liberty in a large state, where they elected representatives. It was acknowledged that the ideal which Rousseau had stated was pure and noble, but it was also, they said, practically useless. Perfection could never be achieved in human affairs, and least of all in politics, wrote Servan. Men had therefore to do what they could for the best in the situation in which they found themselves, rather than pursue chimerical ideals.

'En un mot', he wrote, 'on partira de ce grand principe, que tout ce qui est vraiment nécessaire est bon; et dans une grande et ancienne nation, l'on gardera bien de mettre en question si, pour suivre rigoureusement la volonté générale, il est nécessaire de n'avoir que de petits gouvernements.'[3] It was argued, moreover, that even Rousseau himself regarded his ideal state as chimerical, for he had stated that democracy was fit only for a people of gods. Was it not evident, asked one writer, 'que l'ouvrage de Rousseau ne doit être considéré en grande partie que comme une spéculation, et non pas comme une leçon?'[4]

Not only was the *Social Contract* too theoretical, it was also out of date. Rousseau, it was pointed out, could not possibly have foreseen the great progress of political knowledge and public

[1] See Ch. VI.

[2] Robert, *Le républicanisme*, etc., 1790.

[3] Servan, *Essai sur la formation des assemblées*, etc., 1789, p. 14. The same point of view was expressed by Gudin, Mercier and Robert.

[4] 'Observations sur l'ouvrage de M. de Calonne,' etc., *Mercure de France*, 30 April 1791, p. 196.

enlightenment which would take place after his death. The Revolution had rendered his fears groundless, in Fauchet's view, because in 1789, for the first time, the people were conscious of their rights, and would therefore no longer be the ignorant victims of those who in the past had usurped their sovereignty. These critics of Rousseau placed great emphasis on the new enlightenment of the people, and on the strength of public opinion, which they regarded as fulfilling the important function of guiding the deputies in their formulation of the general will. Brissot, in 1791, explained:

> Rousseau n'aurait pas à ainsi calomnier le système représentatif s'il avait vu à côté, comme en Amérique, un frein aux entreprises des représentants dans les conventions périodiques. Le système représentatif ne devient tyrannique que là où ce frein n'existe pas. Mais les conventions n'étaient pas bien connus aux moment où Rousseau écrivait.[1]

The abbé Fauchet and the Jacobin Robert wished to utilize the new administrative organization of France as the basis for an elaborate system by which the laws could be submitted to primary assemblies throughout the country, and the individual citizens thereby kept in close contact with the activities of their representatives. Thus Robert concluded:

> Il est possible d'introduire un autre espèce de gouvernement représentatif, et qui soit tout à fait cohérente avec les principes de la liberté. Or, en ce sens, Jean-Jacques a erré d'une manière bien funeste à la liberté.[2]

Fauchet excused Rousseau for his pessimism about representation by saying that this was the inevitable effect upon Rousseau's mind of the despotic society in which he lived. He expressed the view that no one would have been more gratified than Rousseau himself, had he lived to see his fears proved groundless.[3]

While, however, it was easy to put aside Rousseau's theories as chimerical and out of date, it was more difficult to answer the

[1] Brissot, *Discours sur les conventions*, 1791, p. 17.

[2] Robert, *Le républicanisme*, etc., 1790, p. 91.

[3] Fauchet, *Bouche de Fer*, 17 January 1791, No. VII, p. 98.

logic of Rousseau's argument that it was not possible for the individual to delegate to another his power of will. In what did sovereignty consist if not in the exercise of the will? How could the general will be expressed in a state too large for the people to express it directly? Gudin accepted Rousseau's definition of the general will, and agreed that in its purity the general will could be expressed only among the virtuous citizens of a small republic. On the other hand he rejected this ideal picture as historically inaccurate, practically unattainable, and in any case irrelevant to the conditions of eighteenth-century France. The French people could in practice only exercise their rights by means of representatives. For supervision of the representative assembly Gudin looked not to primary assemblies but to an upper house, and to the royal power of veto. He devised a careful system of checks and balances, by which the forces of innovation were held in check by the weight of conservatism, and seems to have equated the general will with Aristotle's golden mean.[1]

In 1791, Mercier attempted to reconcile the idea of inalienable sovereignty with the practical necessity of representation by pointing out that although the people delegated sovereign powers to their representatives, nevertheless they retained their fundamental sovereignty because they possessed, in the last resort, the right of insurrection. He rebuked Rousseau for having paid so little attention to this right as a means whereby tyranny could be destroyed and liberty established. The insurrection of 1789, he wrote, had been the first step toward the regeneration of the nation. Mercier was, however, a little nervous about recognizing the right of insurrection as a political principle. He treated it as operating legitimately only in support of the National Assembly; it was a convenient weapon for use against any future attempt at a counter-revolution. At the same time, if a people attempted to exercise the rights which had been delegated to representatives, he argued, orderly government would cease to be possible. The people had in fact said to their representatives: 'Be our legislators, for you know what is best for us.'[2]

[1] Gudin, *Supplément*, etc., 1790.
[2] Mercier, II, vi.

Finally, the conventional revolutionary view of the relation between the sovereignty of the people and the rights of their representatives was put forward in two consecutive articles in the *Mercure de France* in 1791.[1] The author of these articles was particularly concerned to reply to the criticisms of the National Assembly made by Calonne. He also referred to the arguments put forward by other aristocratic and conservative pamphleteers during 1790. These critics of the Revolution had asked how the revolutionaries could reconcile their arguments about the inalienable sovereignty of the people, with their practical recognition of the power of representatives to express the people's will, and how, in recognizing the latter, they could claim to be followers of Rousseau. The answer given by the author of these articles was that Rousseau had been wrong in assuming that sovereign rights could only be exercised by the people. He distinguished between sovereignty, which he agreed belonged inalienably to the nation, and the exercise of sovereign rights, which, he asserted, could be delegated to representatives. He argued that in fact, in a large state these rights had to be delegated, since otherwise they could not be used at all, and it was a contradiction in terms to suppose a right which was incapable of being exercised in practice. In a state too large to permit the assembly of the whole people and the direct exercise of sovereignty, the delegation of sovereign rights was the only alternative to their complete immobilization. Rousseau's theories about representation could not, therefore, he concluded, be taken seriously.

It will be evident that the most severe critics of Rousseau's political theory came from the ranks of the revolutionaries. The main arguments used against the *Social Contract* were practical and empirical. It was argued that Rousseau's theories were too abstract; that they had been rendered obsolete by the development of new political techniques and a politically enlightened public opinion, and that in any case they were quite impractical in eighteenth-century France. While the revolutionaries were prepared to use Rousseau's name when it was convenient, and to appeal to his authority in general terms, they clearly did not regard his theories as having any immediate or direct practical

[1] See p. 108, n. 4, above.

value in the development of their new political institutions. The power of 'doctrine', 'abstract reason' and 'ideologists' over the minds of the revolutionaries has perhaps been exaggerated, and their concern with practical considerations under-estimated.

PART III

The Counter-Revolutionary Rousseau

CHAPTER IX

The Counter-Revolutionary Appeal to Rousseau

An examination has already been made of Isnard's condemnation of the revolutionary concept of the general will, which he regarded as having been derived from the *Social Contract*.[1] Isnard's pamphlet is important because it appears to have been unique: no other pamphlet devoted to the rejection of Rousseau's political theory from an anti-revolutionary point of view and written between 1788–91 has been discovered. Just as the revolutionaries claimed Rousseau as their prophet and patron, so their opponents claimed that the Revolution was condemned 'par chaque ligne du Contrat Social',[2] and even that they, the so-called 'aristocrats', were the true followers of Rousseau.[3] Moreover, anti-revolutionary writers were more thorough in the exposition of Rousseau's theories than revolutionary pamphleteers. They set forward his views in detail, often with extensive quotations and exact references. There was less blatant misinterpretation of Rousseau's theory in aristocratic than in revolutionary pamphlets.

The reasons for this are not difficult to discover. It is not likely that the most scrupulous interpretation of a body of political theory will be found in the writings and speeches of those who are faced with the urgent demands of framing a constitution and solving problems of administration during a period of crises. It has already been shown that the revolutionaries did not base either their theories or their actions on the

[1] See Ch. VI.

[2] Ferrand, *Le dernier coup*, etc., 1790, p. 9.

[3] Lenormant, *Rousseau, aristocrate*, 1790, p. 6.

text of the *Social Contract.* Instead they utilized the prestige of Rousseau's name and picked out, with varying degrees of conscious and unconscious misinterpretation, those ideas which they regarded as useful in furthering particular arguments and policies. On the other hand those who were in opposition, and who found themselves being thrust aside by a movement which they could neither stem nor ride, were less directly affected by the need to adapt political principles to the practical exigencies of government. They could therefore afford to take a more purely philosophical, if not an entirely detached, view of the political theory of Rousseau. Moreover, in the exposition of his principles, the critics of the National Assembly could measure the practical expedients of the revolutionaries against the pure theory by which the latter claimed to be inspired.

A modern parallel springs to mind. In the twentieth century many writers have measured the achievements and failures of the Russian Revolution against what they claim to be the pure theory of Marxism. An important distinction must however be made between the relation of Rousseau's works to the French Revolution, and those of Marx to the Russian Revolution. The works of Marx became the bible of a minority group, organized specifically and exclusively for political and revolutionary purposes. Rousseau's works inspired no political parties, but exercised a profound influence upon men and women whose political opinions were widely different. The political cult of Rousseau was produced by the Revolution, but a legend of Rousseau existed before 1789. The character of this legend was different from that of the Revolution and had no direct relation to the events of 1789. It was based upon an idealized picture of Rousseau's own life and character, and upon the association of Rousseau's life and character with those moral and romantic virtues portrayed in the *Nouvelle Héloise*. This kind of Rousseauism was part of the intellectual heritage of educated men and women at every level of society. In the period 1788–91 the political myth produced by the Revolution had not yet superseded this myth of the great writer and moral teacher in the minds of the opponents of the Revolution, as it was later to do.

In appealing to the political theory of Rousseau, the critics of the Revolution were appealing to the works of a writer whom they regarded as having been wrongly appropriated and outrageously misinterpreted by the revolutionaries. Moreover, as their pamphlets show, this view was not weakened but on the contrary strongly confirmed by their study of Rousseau's political works. As already indicated, many revolutionaries who examined the text of the *Social Contract* with more than usual care were forced to acknowledge that the principles of political justice which Rousseau laid down presented very great difficulties in relation to the practical demands of government in a great state. On the other hand, ample material for the defence of a conservative point of view may be found in Rousseau's political works, and not least in the *Social Contract*. Anti-revolutionary writers could find much with which they were in agreement, and much that could be used to condemn the Revolution out of the mouth and in the words of its own acclaimed prophet. Thus not only did they criticize the Revolution by the standards of the *Social Contract*; they also laid rival claims to be the true followers of Rousseau. One, Lenormant, claimed that had Rousseau been a member of the National Assembly he would have been found sitting among those who were labelled 'aristocrates', and that Rousseau's principles had been consistently maintained and expounded during 1789–90 by—of all people—the great orator of the royalist opposition, the abbé Maury.[1]

It is proposed, in the following chapters, to show how the anti-revolutionary writers endeavoured to prove this close allegiance between their own theories and those of Rousseau. It is, however, important to observe that if the anti-revolutionary interpretation of Rousseau's theories was more carefully stated than that of the revolutionaries, this does not mean that in practice those who criticized the Revolution were less opportunist than their opponents in their use of his ideas. The use of Rousseau's political theory by the anti-revolutionaries belongs mainly to the period 1790–91. Their appeal to Rousseau was therefore made mainly in the context of a retrospective attack upon the National Assembly. This is illustrated by the attack on the representative system. During 1790–91 many anti-revolutionary pamphleteers made much of Rousseau's assertion

[1] Ibid. p. 60.

that sovereignty was incapable of representation, a principle which they claimed to have consistently maintained. They accused the revolutionaries of having betrayed their constituents by forsaking their mandates and having wrongfully usurped the sovereign power. Yet, as already shown in an earlier chapter, Rousseau's authority had not been enlisted to defend the imperative mandate, and no reference had been made to Rousseau, in the discussion of the mandate during the short life of the Estates General or in the early months of the National Assembly.[1] Nor had the defence of the mandate been based on the principle of the inalienable sovereignty of the people, despite d'Antraigues' famous *Mémoire*; on the contrary it was defended by arguments based on the rights of the orders and the provinces, and on historical precedent. Only two pamphlets have been discovered written by conservatives in 1789 and attacking the idea of representation on Rousseauist principles.[2]

It cannot be argued therefore that Rousseau's political theory provided the text upon which the anti-revolutionaries based their practical views upon representation any more than this can be claimed for the revolutionaries. On the contrary, it would appear that, like the revolutionaries themselves, the majority of the opponents and critics of the Revolution did not begin to study Rousseau's political works until the end of 1789. Lenormant, indeed, told his readers explicitly that he was prompted to make his study of the political theory of Rousseau when, to his astonishment, he recognized the bust of Rousseau, with a copy of the *Social Contract* deposited at its base, in the Chamber of the National Assembly.[3] Ferrand similarly informed his readers that he was inspired to study the *Social Contract* by the use of Rousseau's name in debate.[4]

Rousseau's works exercised a twofold attraction upon the critics of the Revolution. His caution and conservatism furnished them with arguments in support of the anti-revolutionary

[1] See Ch. VI.

[2] The first of these is an anonymous pamphlet entitled *Le disciple de Montesquieu à MM. les députés aux États Généraux*, the title of which suggests that it was published before June 1789. The second is Ferrand's *Adresse d'un citoyen très-actif*, which was published at the end of 1789, and republished in 1790.

[3] Lenormant, *Rousseau, aristocrate*, 1790, p. 3.

[4] Ferrand, *Adresse d'un citoyen*, etc., 1789, pp. 1–4.

case, and at the same time, to the extent to which the great philosopher's name was honoured by the adherents of the Revolution, his political works could be regarded as a useful means by which the Revolutionaries could be hoist with their own petard.

In the following sections it is proposed to analyse the views expressed in thirty-six pamphlets, articles and published opinions in which the writers appeal to the authority of Rousseau to criticize the National Assembly or to condemn the Revolution as a whole. Of this number, five pamphlets are devoted specifically to an examination of the principles and practices of the revolutionaries in the light of Rousseau's political theory, in order to show how directly they contradicted each other.

One pamphlet is devoted to showing that the revolutionaries were acting not only contrary to the principles stated by Rousseau, but to those of other reputable philosophers as well. In the remaining tracts, Rousseau's theories are examined in varying degrees of detail in the course of arguments directed against the Revolution. The majority of these pamphlets, a total of twenty-two, were published in 1790. One only was published in 1788, six in 1789 and seven in 1791.

The main purposes of these pamphlets was to show that the revolutionaries had misunderstood and misinterpreted Rousseau's political theories which, their authors claimed, were directly contrary to those upon which the revolutionaries had based their actions. 'Un double reproche, ce me semble, à faire à nos représentants philosophes,' wrote one, 'c'est d'avoir dédaigné nos plus grands législateurs, tels que Montesquieu, Mably même, et surtout d'avoir mal interpreté le profond Rousseau.'[1] Another accused the revolutionaries of appealing to Rousseau's authority simply in order to strengthen their own. They needed, he wrote, a respectable screen behind which to impose their views upon the nation. 'Si Rousseau vivait,' he asserted, 'on se garderait bien de profaner ses maximes . . . parce qu'ils n'ont rien fait qui ne soit absolument contraire à tout ce qu'il a dit sur la matière des gouvernements.'[2]

[1] Anon., *Apologie de la noblesse*, etc., 1790, p. 59. See also de Bourdeille, *Réflexions*, etc., 1790, p. 141; Anon., *Adresse aux Français*, etc., 1790, p. 27.

[2] Anon., *Le dernier cri*, etc., 1791, p. 82.

It was the *Social Contract* in particular that the revolutionaries were accused of having misinterpreted. They were deceiving themselves by appealing to Rousseau's authority, for, 'tous les principes du Contrat Social déposent contre eux'. Maury had stated that the revolutionaries 'ne cessent de s'étayer des assertions du Contrat Social de J. J. Rousseau, et leur condamnation s'y trouve à chaque page.'[1] Ferrand claimed that the National Assembly had distorted Rousseau's obvious intentions by invoking his authority to support decrees which were formally condemned by every line of the *Social Contract*.[2] Every page of the *Social Contract*, he wrote, was in contradiction with the work of the National Assembly.[3] One anonymous author asserted that all Europe was scandalized by the praises sung to Rousseau in an Assembly whose every decree was pronounced as null by the *Social Contract*.[4] The author of a series of articles on the National Assembly published in the journal *L'Année Littéraire* remarked that a journalist who had recently hailed the *Social Contract* as the source of the new political faith, must surely have neglected to have read this work for, he asserted, 'les idées de J. J. Rousseau sont presque en tout diamétralement opposées aux dogmes de notre nouvelle foi politique.'[5]

The anti-revolutionary writers pointed out, further, that the *Social Contract* was not intended to contain political proposals. They argued that it was a purely theoretical work; a piece of philosophical speculation, 'un beau système', as Lenormant explained, which Rousseau himself admitted to be incapable of being put into practice. Rousseau, they argued, was writing in the abstract of men's rights; he was not preparing a practical guide to legislation.[6] The *Social Contract* ought not therefore in the view of these writers to have been regarded as a kind of political or legislative text book. 'Rousseau, écrivain, ne pouvait commander que la vérité' wrote the Marquis Ducrest, 'mais

[1] Anon., *Le Réveil des Rois*, etc., 1791, see title-page.

[2] Ferrand, *Le dernier coup*, etc., 1790, p. 9.

[3] Ferrand, *Addresse d'un citoyen*, etc., 1789, pp. 1–4.

[4] Anon., *Catéchisme Anti-constitutionnel*, etc., 1790, p. 4.

[5] Anon., *L'Assemblée Nationale*, 1789, lett. xvii, pp. 223–4.

[6] Anon., *Première lettre à M. de la Cretelle*, 1789, p. 13; D'Antraigues, *Quelle est la situation*, etc., 1790, p. 39; Lenormant, *Rousseau, aristocrate*, etc., 1790, p. 97; Maury, *Opinion sur la souveraineté*, etc., 1790, p. 29; Anon., *Le Naviget Anticyras*, etc., 1790, pp. 120, 121.

Rousseau orateur public, aurait commandé l'erreur.'[1] Another writer observed that it was misguided to put forward Rousseau's political principles as practical proposals, for he was purely a theorist, and never intended his works to be used in this way.[2]

In view of the revolutionary misuse of the *Social Contract*, one aristocratic admirer of Rousseau's works took it upon himself to prevent any further distortions of Rousseau's political theories by destroying the manuscript sequel to the *Social Contract*, which he claimed had been entrusted to him by the author. D'Antraigues conveyed this information to his readers in a note to his pamphlet *Quelle est la situation de l'Assemblée Nationale?*, published in 1791. He described how in this document Rousseau had set out to show, as he had promised in the *Social Contract*,[3] that the advantages of the small state could be combined with the external strength of a great Empire, by means of the system of confederations. According to d'Antraigues, Rousseau's manuscript was unfinished, but it contained thirteen chapters already written, a sketch of the general scheme which the author proposed to follow, and notes on certain points which Rousseau proposed to develop more fully.

D'Antraigues related how, carried away by enthusiasm in July 1789, he had thought that it would be to his countrymen's advantage if this document were published. He was, however, dissuaded from this course of action by a friend, who warned him that such a work would inevitably be seized upon by the very people who would make the most dangerous use of it. Such people, his friend averred, would disregard whatever it contained of value, but they would pick out whatever was impractical or dangerous, or whatever could be used against the monarchy and the established order. D'Antraigues concluded that these warnings had been borne out by the use made of the *Social Contract*, and congratulated himself for having followed his friend's advice. 'Ah! que j'ai bien reçu le prix de cette déférence, grand Dieu!' he exclaimed, 'que n'auraient-ils pas

[1] Ducrest, *Essai sur les principes*, etc., 1789, p. 8.

[2] Anon., *Première lettre à M. de la Cretelle*, 1789, p. 13.

[3] *C.S.* III, ch. xv; Vaughan, II, 102.

fait de cet écrit? comme ils l'auraient fouillé ceux qui, dédaignant d'étudier les écrits de ce grand homme, ont dénaturé et avili ses principes; ceux qui n'ont pas vu que le Contrat Social, ouvrage isolé et abstrait, n'était applicable à aucun peuple de l'univers.'[1]

Two writers presented Rousseau as repudiating his *Social Contract* from the fields of Elysium. One of these described how, on Mirabeau's arrival in the next world, Rousseau, acting as his guide, was made to protest that the National Assembly, 'qui se vante de rien faire que d'après mes écrits, a fait bien souvent des sottises . . . !' He was pictured expressing regret for having written the *Social Contract* and lamenting that 'les semences précieuses qu'il renferme ont produit, chez un peuple qu'il aime, des fruits si amers qu'ils deviendront des poisons mortels, si le roi et les amis de la monarchie ne rassemblent pas enfin toutes leurs forces pour s'opposer à ces effets désastreux.'[2]

It is important to emphasize that although anti-revolutionary writers deplored the use made of the *Social Contract* by their adversaries, they did not condemn the *Social Contract* itself. The majority perceived that in the *Social Contract* Rousseau distinguished between ideal principles and practical possibilities. Their main complaint against the revolutionary interpreters of Rousseau was that the latter ignored the practical advice given by Rousseau in order to concentrate on those abstract principles which Rousseau held to be capable of practical realization only in very special circumstances, and perhaps never fully realizable in any.

This does not mean, however, that the critics of the Revolution left the *Social Contract* to its revolutionary fate and concentrated upon works of obvious conservatism. On the contrary, the *Social Contract* provided most important ammunition for the aristocratic and conservative armoury. Lenormant used a total of forty-nine quotations and references from Rousseau's works to show that Rousseau's political theory was directly opposed to the legislation of the National Assembly. Of this number, twenty-nine were drawn from the *Social Contract*, as against twenty-two from the *Considérations*, eleven from the *Lettres*

[1] See above, pp. 59, n. 2, and 122, n. 1.

[2] *Les Sabats Jacobites*, 1791, Nos. 33, 34, pp. 117, 126–7.

écrites de la Montagne, three from the *Discours sur l'Économie politique*, two from the *Second Discourse* and one each from Rousseau's introductions to the *Polysinodie* and the *Projet de Paix perpetuelle*. Ferrand's pamphlet *Adresse d'un citoyen très actif* consisted of thirty-one questions put to the National Assembly, in each of which the deputies were asked to explain the obvious inconsistency between the principles upon which they based their legislation and the principles set forward in specific passages of the *Social Contract*. D'Escherny, in his *Correspondance d'un habitant de Paris*, analysed what he regarded as the main principles of the *Social Contract* and showed that none of these had been accepted by the revolutionaries. He concluded that Rousseau's political thought had in fact had no influence on the Revolution.

The anonymous author of the pamphlet *Le Réveil des Rois* made thirty references to and quotations from Rousseau's works, of which twenty-one were from the *Social Contract*. Quotations from the *Social Contract* predominated in two articles which appeared in the journal *Les Actes des Apôtres*, in which the anti-revolutionary case against the National Assembly was expounded. A total of ten quotations from the *Social Contract* were used by the author of a pamphlet entitled *Catéchisme anti-constitutionnel*. Similarly, the author of a pamphlet entitled *Le dernier cri de la vérité sur la Révolution française*, who condemned the Assembly on the basis of Rousseau's political theory, made considerable use of the *Social Contract*. Thus the *Social Contract* was used as an anti-revolutionary weapon, and it was used with both subtlety and skill.

Rousseau was pictured by counter-revolutionary writers as a conservative who showed extreme caution toward any suggestion that change, particularly violent change, could improve men's lot. He had believed that the laws might be improved, but that since in any case abuses were inevitable, it was pointless to sacrifice well-tried institutions for the uncertainty of new ones.[1] The degeneration of states was inevitable with time, and the possibility of arresting corruption remote. Indeed, it was

[1] See *C.G.P.*, Vaughan, II, 426 ff. Quoted by: Lenormant, *Rousseau, aristocrate*, 1790, p. 69 ff.; Ferrand, *Le Dernier Coup*, etc., 1790, p. 9; Anon., *Le Tableau de rapprochement*, 1790, pp. 15–16; Anon., *A l'Assemblée prétendue nationale*, 1790, p. 56.

actually dangerous to try to change customs which had formed men's social and moral habits over the centuries. Thus, on Rousseau's reasoning, if a people had a bad government then it was better to choose the lesser of two evils and resign themselves to their lot.[1]

Anti-revolutionary writers dismissed the popular view of Rousseau as the apostle of liberty. He was presented as the stalwart defender of custom and tradition, who doubted the possibility that a greater degree of liberty could be enjoyed by the majority of people. It was pointed out that in the *Social Contract* he warned his readers that liberty was not the fruit of all climates,[2] and that in the dedication to the *Second Discourse* he asserted that liberty was not for a people that had once become accustomed to masters[3]; on the contrary, it was the jealousy of the people against great men which had been the main cause of the downfall of empires.[4] The warnings which Rousseau gave to the Poles about the dangers of a too rapid enfranchisement of their serfs, and his assertion that liberty was too dearly bought at the cost of human life, were quoted in relation to the disorderly behaviour of the French peasantry and townspeople.[5]

[1] See *J.P.*, Vaughan, I, 415, 416. Quoted by: Ferrand, *Le dernier coup*, etc., 1790, pp. 11–12; Anon., *L'abus des mots*, 1790, Appendix. See *C.S.*, Bk. III, Ch. x, Vaughan, II, 54, 56. Quoted by: Ferrand, *Adresse d'un citoyen*, etc., 1789, pp. 17–18; Anon., *De la nécessité de montrer*, etc., 1790, p. 10; Anon., *Adresse à tous les membres*, etc., 1791, p. 11. See: *L.M.*, Vaughan, II, 54–56. Quoted by Anon., *L'abus des mots*, 1790, Appendix.

[2] See *C.S.*, Bk. III, Ch. VIII, Vaughan, vol. II, p. 82. Quoted by: Ferrand, *Adresse d'un citoyen*, etc., 1789, pp. 22–3; Anon., *Le Tableau de rapprochement*, 1790, p. 25.

[3] See *D.G.*, *D.I.*, Vaughan, p. 127. Quoted by: Lenormant, *Rousseau, aristocrate*, 1790, pp. 75–6; Demarest, *Coup d'œil impartiel*, etc., 1790, p. 14; Maury, *Opinion sur la souveraineté*, etc., 1790, p. 239; Anon., *Le Tableau de rapprochement*, 1790, p. 25; Anon., *De la nécessité de montrer*, etc., 1790, p. 12; Anon., *Qui est-ce donc qui gagne?*, etc., 1790, p. 24; Anon., *Apologie de la noblesse*, etc., 1790, p. 58; Anon., *Le Réveil des Rois*, etc., 1791, p. 33.

[4] See *C.S.*, IV, ch. V, Vaughan, II, 118–19. Quoted by: Demarest, *Coup d'œil impartiel*, etc., 1790, p. 10; Anon., *La Monarchie Vengée*, etc., 1791, pp. xlii–xliii.

[5] See *C.G.P.*, Vaughan, II, 445. Quoted by: Lenormant, *Rousseau, aristocrate*, 1790, p. 86; Malouet, *Sur le discours du Roi*, etc., 1790, p. 262; Anon., *De la nécessité de montrer*, etc., 1790, p. 3; Anon., *Qui est-ce donc qui gagne?*, etc., 1790, p. 24; Anon., *Le Tableau de rapprochement*, 1790, p. 18; Anon., *La Monarchie vengée*, etc., 1791, p. 55.

Rousseau was presented as the upholder of traditional government. His name was associated with those of Bossuet and Montaigne,[1] and particularly with Montesquieu,[2] as supporting monarchy and the necessity for intermediate orders in the large monarchical state. Why was it, one writer asked, that the revolutionaries had appropriated Rousseau as their oracle and yet rejected Montesquieu, when Rousseau was in fact the disciple of Montesquieu, the greater part of whose principles he adopted?[3] It was pointed out that Rousseau stated quite clearly that he did not wish to live in a country whose laws were newly instituted, and that in his own lifetime he had preferred to go into exile rather than become the centre of public disturbance and controversy.[4] Ferrand reminded his readers that Rousseau rejected the mild plan of reform put forward by the abbé de Saint Pierre on the ground that it was dangerous to disturb the customs of the great mass of the people. How much more horified would he have been, he asked, if it had been suggested that the principles contained in the *Social Contract* should have been applied to France? Rousseau, said Ferrand, could hardly be regarded as a man of timid imagination, but he shrank from the idea of so far-reaching a reform, even though he acknowledged the advantages of the plan put forward in the *Polysinodie*. The revolutionaries, on the contrary, were lightheartedly undertaking to put into practice drastic changes according to a plan which was riddled with obvious faults.[5]

To picture Rousseau alive in the first three years of the Revolution and to describe his reactions was a favourite device. The anonymous author of an article in the journal *Les Actes des*

[1] Demarest, *Coup d'œil impartiel*, etc., 1790, pp. 10, 11. Montlosier, *L'art de constituer les peuples*, 1790, p. 19. Anon., *Catéchisme anti-constitutionnel*, etc., 1790 passim. Anon., *Qui est-ce donc qui gagne?*, etc., 1790, p. 22. Anon., *Adresse à tous les membres*, etc., 1791, p. 15.

[2] Anon., *Le disciple de Montesquieu*, etc., 1789, pp. 33, 94. De Bourdeille, *Réflexions*, etc., 1790, p. 141. Maury, *Opinion sur la souveraineté*, etc., 1790, passim. Anon., *Adresse aux Français*, etc., 1790, p. 27. Anon., *La décadence de l'Empire français*, 1790, p. 20. Anon., *Le dernier cri*, etc., 1790, see Second Examen. Anon., *Lisez ceci bons Français*, 1790, passim. Anon., *Adresse à tous les membres*, etc., 1791, p. 15.

[3] Anon., *Le dernier cri*, etc., 1791, p. 89.

[4] See *D.G.*, *D.I.*, Vaughan, I, 126. Quoted by Lenormant, *Rousseau, aristocrate*, 1790, pp. 73, 75–7.

[5] Ferrand, *Le dernier coup*, etc., 1790, p. 12. See also Lenormant, *Rousseau, aristocrate*, 1790, pp. 90–4.

Apôtres envisaged a debate between Rousseau and the members of the National Assembly. Rousseau was shown advising against any changes in the political and social life of France, and attempting to moderate the zeal of the Assembly. All was in vain. The deputies decided that their hero had become an old dotard whose brain was enfeebled by age, while Rousseau, trembling with horror at the proposals put forward, finally took to his heels and fled.[1] Lenormant argued that had Rousseau been alive he would certainly have been opposed to the Revolution. Had it been impossible to have prevented the Revolution, then he would have taken the only course open to one of his views. He would have sided with the aristocratic minority in the Assembly, and 'loin d'être l'auteur de la Révolution de 1789, en eut été l'adversaire et le fléau'. By 1790, he would no doubt already have joined the stream of émigrés who had been forced to leave France in their hundreds in order to save their lives.[2]

Arguments of this kind were not uncommon in 1790–1. In the journal *Les Actes des Apôtres* attention was drawn to the claim made by the critics of the National Assembly that they were the true followers of Rousseau. The editors summarized these arguments which, they claimed, were widely current. They were clearly sympathetic to them, although they put them forward with mock disapproval, and only, they claimed, in order that their legislators might be aware of the existence of such treachery.[3] The use of Rousseauist arguments by the opponents of the Assembly was also noted by other writers who had less reason to draw attention to the conservative utilization of Rousseau's political principles. 'Bien des gens croient que Rousseau a condamné d'avance plusieurs opérations de l'Assemblée Nationale,' wrote one. He concluded, however, that 'ils ont, sans doute, mal saisi les opinions de ce philosophe,

[1] Anon., *Le Tableau de rapprochement*, 1790, p. 19. See also Anon., *Lettre d'un impartiel à un anonyme*, 1790, p. 3.

[2] Lenormant, *Rousseau, aristocrate*, 1790, pp. 5, 74.

[3] Anon., 'Sophismes politiques', 1790. This article appeared in No. 52 of *Actes des Apôtres*. The journal was founded by Peltier, and its contributors referred to themselves as 'the forty-five apostles'. Only a few of them are known, including Champcenetz, Rivarol, Mirabeau, Montlosier, Bergasse and Peltier himself. Hatin described this journal as 'Une des feuilles royalistes les plus célèbres, et de toutes celles de l'époque la plus spirituelle et la plus piquante'.

ou les circonstances de la Révolution.'[1] It remains to consider, in the study of the detailed arguments of the anti-revolutionaries, whether the latter had indeed misunderstood the opinions of the philosopher as was asserted.

[1] 'Hommage de la nation à J. J. Rousseau', see *Mercure de France,* 12 February 1791, pp. 49–54, and p. 53, n.

CHAPTER X

The Attack on the Assembly

A CONSTANT theme of anti-revolutionary pamphlets was the accusation levelled against the deputies of the National Assembly that they had wrongfully usurped power by forsaking the mandates of their constituents and departing from the *cahiers*. Perhaps the most important single work in which this subject was developed was Calonne's *De l'état de la France, présent et à venir*, which, published first in October 1790, had run into six editions by March 1791. This argument also appeared in a great number of pamphlets in which it was not associated with the political theory of Rousseau. The important pamphlet of Ferrand, for example, entitled *Nullité et despotisme de l'assemblée prétendue nationale* of which three editions were published in 1790, attacked the departure of the deputies from their mandates without reference to Rousseau's views on representation. Nevertheless, Rousseau's condemnation of representation was utilized by many anti-revolutionary pamphleteers. They pointed out that the revolutionary concept of representation was the antithesis of that of Rousseau. One writer remarked upon the irony of an Assembly paying tribute to a philosopher whose works condemned the very principle of its existence as well as all its actions.[1] Another asked, 'N'est-il pas plaisant que l'homme réputé le plus grand génie en politique regarde notre Assemblée Nationale comme un rejeton de ce gouvernement féodal que l'Assemblée Nationale s'efforce d'extirper?'[2]

Three main arguments can be traced in the attacks upon the

[1] Anon., *Catéchisme anti-constitutionnel*, 1790, p. 4.

[2] Anon., *L'Assemblée Nationale*, 1789, let. xvii, p. 225.

National Assembly. In the first place the attention of the revolutionaries was drawn to Rousseau's fundamental precept of the inalienable character of sovereignty. Secondly, it was argued that according to Rousseau's principles the people's deputies were not their representatives but their 'mandataires'. Thirdly, the deputies were accused of having betrayed their mandates and of having substituted their particular wills for the general will expressed in the *cahiers*. It is, of course, not the case that all those who followed and applied Rousseau's argument, beginning with the inalienable character of sovereignty and ending with the inevitable usurpation of power by representatives, necessarily accepted Rousseau's first principles. On the contrary, two writers explicitly denied that the people were sovereign,[1] and the majority relegated the idea of popular sovereignty to that realm of ideal principles of whose practical value Rousseau himself was doubtful outside the hypothetical conditions of the small republic. This did not prevent them from attacking their opponents according to Rousseauist theory. They repeated Rousseau's assertion that in representative government he could see no more than masters and slaves. They pointed out that he regarded representation as a vestige of the absurd and degrading system of feudalism, and that he mocked at the English for believing themselves to be free when in fact they were free only during their elections.[2]

Lenormant claimed that from 1789 onwards the aristocrats in the National Assembly had consistently followed Rousseau in maintaining that sovereignty could not be represented.[3] The abbé Maury argued that whereas a small nation could so constitute its government as to enable the people to exercise a direct influence on legislation, a great nation could not. It had necessarily to fall back upon either confederations or representation. And Rousseau, from whose works the deputies of the

[1] Maury, *Opinion sur la souveraineté*, 1790, pp. 113, 134–5. Anon., *Le dernier cri*, etc., 1791. See *Premier Examen.*

[2] Anon., *L'Assemblée Nationale*, 1789, let. xvii, p. 224. Anon., *Le disciple de Montesquieu*, etc., 1789, p. 94. Lenormant, *Rousseau, aristocrate*, 1790, p. 41 ff. Maury, *Opinion sur la souveraineté*, 1790, pp. 77–8. Anon., *Catéchisme anti-constitutionnel*, 1790, p. 13. Anon., *A l'Assemblée prétendue nationale*, 1790, p. 49. Anon., *Le Réveil des Rois*, 1791, p. 15.

[3] Lenormant, *Rousseau, aristocrate*, 1790, p. 24.

National Assembly chose only the exaggerations, wrote Maury, proved perfectly in the *Social Contract* that not only were the people not sovereign, but they were no longer free when they had established a representative government.[1] Rousseau, it was said, held that deputies were simply 'mandataires', bound by their mandates and obliged to account for their actions to their constituents, who were urged to subject their deputies' reports to the closest scrutiny. Only in this way, it was argued, did he believe it possible to prevent the substitution of the particular wills of the deputies for the general will of the nation.[2]

Calonne described the role of the deputies as follows:

Députés de chaque portion du royaume, vous êtes porteurs du voeu de chaque assemblée, sur les différents points constitutionnels compris dans son instruction, et comme membres du Corps représentatif de la Nation, vous devez rapprocher et faire concorder les vœux de toutes les assemblées, pour en tirer l'expression de la volonté générale; . . .[3]

One writer quoted from the *Social Contract* in relation to the *cahiers*,

Ôtez des volontés particulières; les plus et les moins qui s'entre-détruisent, reste pour somme des différences la volonté générale.[4]

Another asserted that the government of France was already decided in the instructions given to the deputies.[5] If those who were sent to establish the well-being of France on the basis of a sound constitution had followed their instructions, as they had sworn to do, wrote one pamphleteer, then the constitution would have been determined according to the majority of *cahiers*, and the deputies would have exercised a power which

[1] Maury, *Opinion sur la souveraineté*, 1790, pp. 76, 125, 147–8.

[2] Anon., *Lettre de J. J. Rousseau*, etc., 1789, p. 4. Calonne, *De l'état de France*, etc., 1790, pp. 338, 341. Lenormant, *Rousseau, aristocrate*, 1790, p. 45. Anon., *Qui est-ce donc qui gagne?*, etc., 1790, p. 22. Anon., *Sophismes politiques*, 1790, p. 7. Anon., *Le Tableau de rapprochement*, 1790, pp. 54–6. Anon., *Adresse à tous les membres*, etc., 1791, p. 14. Anon., *Le dernier cri*, etc., 1791, p. 83. Anon., *La Monarchie vengée*, etc., 1791, p. 52. Anon., *Le Réveil des Rois*, 1791, pp. 4–5.

[3] Calonne, *De l'état de France*, etc., 1790, p. 338.

[4] Anon., *Le Réveil des Rois*, 1791, p. 5.

[5] Anon., *La Monarchie vengée*, etc., 1791, p. 52.

would have been legitimate.[1] The deputies however misconstrued their mandates and went beyond the instructions contained in them.[2] They were charged with specific tasks; they were not entitled to embark upon wholesale 'régénération'. In departing from the *cahiers*, it was alleged, the deputies had violated Rousseau's principles in two senses, for the *cahiers* were in complete accord with Rousseau's theories in recognizing the necessity for the traditional forms of monarchial government in France.[3]

Calonne quoted Rousseau to show that having departed from their instructions the deputies had rendered the very existence of the Assembly invalid.[4] Another writer asserted that in destroying one government and replacing it with another, the deputies had made necessary a new social compact.[5] They were accused of deceiving the people by continuing to use Rousseauist phraseology when in fact they had offended against the first and fundamental principle of Rousseau's political theory.[6] Malouet protested against the use of Rousseauist ideas which, he said, though perfectly logical within the context of Rousseau's political theory, were quite out of keeping with the conditions of eighteenth-century France.[7] Maury accused the deputies of using the phrase 'sovereignty of the people' in order to cloak their own usurpation. In fact, he wrote, the people had less real power than the *rois fainéants* of the first dynasty whom the Palace Mayors used to lead out for exhibition once a year. His purpose in his *Opinion sur la souveraineté du peuple* was to attack the theory of popular sovereignty. He admitted that he did not agree with Rousseau's theory of sovereignty, but he nevertheless pointed out that Rousseau's concept of the indivisible and inalienable character of sovereignty was completely falsified by the claim of the National Assembly to be acting according to his principles.

[1] Anon., *Sophismes politiques*, 1790, p. 6.
[2] Calonne, *De l'état de France*, etc., 1790, p. 334.
[3] Anon., *Lettre de J. J. Rousseau*, etc., 1789, pp. 4–5. Anon., *Le Réveil des Rois*, 1791, p. 7.
[4] Calonne, *De l'état de France*, etc., 1790, p. 243.
[5] Anon., *Le Réveil des Rois*, 1791, pp. 6, 15.
[6] Anon., *Le dernier cri*, etc., 1791, p. 82.
[7] Malouet, *Sur l'acte constitutionnel*, 1791, p. 8.

Thus the Assembly was accused of having committed a double crime. Not only had the deputies betrayed their mandates, but in order to justify this crime against the nation they had distorted Rousseau's philosophy and used it to hide their usurpations. Ferrand observed that many people held the view that soon every man in France would be able to read. If that was so, he wrote, then when the people came to read the *Social Contract* the National Assembly would find itself in difficulties. Although the Assembly had shown a masterly adroitness in reconciling irreconcilables, nevertheless they could not escape from Rousseau's condemnation of representation. Book III, Ch. XV, he said, was the touchstone of the Assembly's claim to follow Rousseau's principle; and this chapter, Ferrand asserted 'sappe l'Assemblée par la base; il lui ôte jusqu'au droit d'exister'.[1]

Apart from discussing the wider problem of representation in relation to Rousseau's principles, many conservative writers also compared the character and role of the National Assembly with that ascribed by Rousseau to the Legislator in the *Social Contract*. Rousseau's description of the great man who was capable of taking upon himself the task of laying the foundations of society was seized upon by the critics of the Assembly, who pointed out that they could hardly recognize this superhuman genius in the self-appointed legislators of France. The impudence of the members of the Assembly in undertaking so confidently the regeneration of a nation already corrupt, a task which Rousseau himself had regarded as impossible, and which Plato had refused to touch, was emphasized.[2] Rousseau had said that it would need gods to give men good laws, but France, said one pamphleteer, was in the hands of men without principles, without religion, and without even experience.[3] Nor could they be regarded as disinterested, a quality upon which Rousseau had insisted. The legislators of France, observed

[1] Ferrand, *Adresse d'un citoyen*, etc., 1790, pp. 39, 48.

[2] Ferrand, *Adresse d'un citoyen*, etc., 1789, p. 11. Anon., *L'Assemblée Nationale*, 1789, Let. vii, p. 84. Anon., *Catéchisme anti-constitutionnel*, 1790, p. 5. Anon., *Sophismes politiques*, 1790, p. 7. Anon., *Le Tableau de rapprochement*, 1790, pp. 14–15. Anon., *Le Réveil des Rois*, 1791, p. 10.

[3] Anon., *Catéchisme anti-constitutionnel*, 1790, p. 6. See also Anon., *Le Réveil des Rois*, 1791, p. 10, and Anon., *L'Assemblée Nationale*, 1789, Let. vii, p. 84.

Ferrand, with bitter sarcasm, saw, like Rousseau's legislator, all the passions of men, but after having attended several of their sessions one could hardly believe that they did not share them also.[1] Rousseau, it was alleged, would not have recognized his legislator in the National Assembly, but how easily he would have recognized his usurper.[2]

Not only the character of the Assembly but its method of procedure was compared with that of Rousseau's legislator. Rousseau had followed Montesquieu. The National Assembly, however, according to its Rousseauist critics, had framed laws on abstract principles and had attempted to force upon the French nation institutions which the character of the people could not support.[3]

Again, Rousseau had asserted that whoever drew up the laws could have no right of legislation. This meant that the same individual, or group of individuals, could not both draw up a constitution and also claim the power to apply it. Secondly, Rousseau had laid it down that no law could be regarded as valid which had not received the sanction of the nation. Thus the Assembly was regarded as having confused and retained in its own hands the constituent power and the power of legislation, and of having usurped the sovereign right of the people to ratify the laws. Let us consider the arguments used by conservative writers in relation to these two accusations.

'Pour exécuter l'ouvrage de la législation,' wrote one author, 'il faut trouver une autorité qui ne soit rien.' If this principle was not followed, then, as Rousseau foresaw, the legislator would become despotic.[4] Rousseau had shown that where the sovereign and constituent powers were vested in the same hands, particular passions would inevitably triumph over the general will.[5] Ferrand wrote that when he read this passage

[1] Ferrand, *Adresse d'un citoyen*, etc., 1789, p. 12. Compare Lenormant, *Rousseau, aristocrate*, 1790, p. 42.

[2] Ferrand, *Adresse d'un citoyen*, etc., 1789, p. 16. See also: Lenormant, *Rousseau, aristocrate*, 1790, p. 78. Anon., *Sophismes politiques*, 1790, p. 6. Anon., *Le Tableau de rapprochement*, 1790, pp. 41–2.

[3] Lenormant, *Rousseau, aristocrate*, 1790, pp. 42, 99 ff. Anon., *Catéchisme anti-constitutionnel*, 1790, pp. 8, 26, 27. Anon., *Sophismes politiques*, 1790, p. 7. Anon., *Le Tableau de rapprochement*, 1790, pp. 15–16, 25–6.

[4] Anon., *Sophismes politiques*, 1790, p. 5.

[5] Anon., *Le Réveil des Rois*, 1790, p. 28.

in the *Social Contract* its relevance to the National Assembly struck him forcibly. If the Assembly continued to try to command both laws and men, he wrote, then the laws would simply become the instrument of passion, perpetuating injustice. He quoted the passage in which Rousseau warned that when men turn their attention from general to particular ends, the laws cease to be just. In Rousseau's chapter on the legislator, Ferrand pointed out: 'On trouve à la fois dans l'ouvrage de la législation deux choses qui semblent incompatibles: une entreprise au-dessus de la force humaine, et pour l'exécuter, une autorité qui n'est rien.' The Assembly, however, had not troubled about this apparent inconsistency, for, said Ferrand: 'Après avoir formé une entreprise peut-être au-dessus de ses forces, l'assemblée, pour l'exécuter, a pris toute l'autorité qui était dans le royaume. . . .'[1]

Attention was drawn to Rousseau's statement that Rome suffered under tyranny and was brought to the verge of destruction simply because the constituent and sovereign powers were vested in the same hands.[2]

In all conflicts arising out of the substitution of new laws for the old ones, whether with the other branches of government, or with the corporate bodies of the Ancien Régime, the National Assembly had become the self-appointed judge in its own case, and, as Rousseau had perceived would be inevitable in such circumstances, it had judged according to its own interests, or, in the words of Ferrand, 'dans le sens de la Révolution'.[3]

The result had been that all other branches of government had been reduced to a position of subservience to the Assembly. The latter had concerned itself with administrative, judicial and executive affairs which should have been regarded as distinct and independent of the constituent power. 'L'Assemblée a certainement la prétension d'être la volonté générale. Cependant sa sollicitude paternelle la porte à s'occuper journellement d'une multitude d'objets particuliers,' wrote Ferrand.[4]

[1] Ferrand, *Adresse d'un citoyen*, etc., 1789, pp. 10–16.
[2] Anon., *Adresse à tous les membres*, etc., 1791, p. 10.
[3] Ferrand, *Le dernier coup*, etc., 1790, p. 15.
[4] Ferrand, *Adresse d'un citoyen*, etc., 1789, pp. 13–14. See also: Clermont Tonnerre,

Rousseau's insistence on the necessity of ratification of laws by the people was constantly emphasized by critics of the National Assembly.[1] Lenormant denied that he would have accepted the addresses of adherence received by the Assembly as expressing the general will and therefore as taking the place of ratification.[2] It was argued that the Assembly was incompetent to take any final decision, since according to Rousseau's principles all its acts were invalid without ratification by the free suffrage of the people.[3] One writer complained that the fate of the nation was at the mercy of a majority of five or six in the Assembly, but that twenty-six million men were deprived of that right of ratifying the laws, claimed for them by Rousseau.[4] Ferrand compared the powers which the Assembly had claimed with those of the decemvirs described by Rousseau in his chapter on the legislator, and pointed out that the deputies were not only following, but even surpassing, the example of the Roman tyrants.[5]

How far can these writers be regarded as putting forward in good faith the demand for a ratification of the laws, or how far should they be regarded as using this argument drawn from the *Social Contract* simply to embarrass their opponents? It has already been pointed out that a number of writers who appealed to Rousseau's political theory to attack the National Assembly nevertheless rejected Rousseau's principle of sovereignty, while others insisted that this principle was not intended by the author to have any relevance in eighteenth-century France. Nevertheless, we find that the same writers who denied the validity or practicability of the theory of inalienable sove-

---

Sur l'influence le Monarque doit avoir, etc., 1790, p. 5. Ferrand, *Le dernier coup*, etc., 1790, p. 3 ff. Lenormant, *Rousseau, aristocrate*, 1790, pp. 41–2. Maury, *Sur le droit de choisir les juges*, 1790, p. 22. Anon., *Sophismes politiques*, 1790, pp. 5, 6. Anon., *Le Tableau de rapprochement*, 1790, pp. 28–9, 30, 45, 52–3. Anon., *Le dernier cri*, etc., 1791, p. 83.

[1] Ferrand, *Adresse d'un citoyen*, etc., 1789, p. 39. Lenormant, *Rousseau, aristocrate*, 1790, pp. 44–5. Anon., *Catéchisme anti-constitutionnel*, 1790, pp. 14, 33. Anon., *De la nécessité de montrer*, etc., 1790, p. 6. Anon., *Sophismes politiques*, 1790, p. 5. Anon., *Le Tableau de rapprochement*, 1790, pp. 45–6. Anon., *Le Réveil des Rois*, 1791, p. 7.

[2] Lenormant, *Rousseau, aristocrate*, 1790, pp. 48–9.

[3] Anon., *Le dernier cri*, etc., 1791, p. 84. Anon., *Le Réveil des Rois*, 1791, p. 15.

[4] Anon., *Catéchisme anti-constitutionnel*, 1790, p. 33.

[5] Ferrand, *Adresse d'un citoyen*, etc., 1789, p. 14.

reignty, also inveighed against the despotism of the Assembly and emphasized Rousseau's principle of ratification.

Calonne, for example, insisted that a system by which the representatives of the people made themselves independent of their constituents was unacceptable in any form of government. He quoted Rousseau's statement that, 'Toute loi que le peuple en personne n'a pas ratifiée est nulle, ce n'est point une loi'. Like other critics of the Assembly, however, Calonne put forward no constructive proposals as to how ratification should be put into practice. Indeed, after having made the above quotation from the *Social Contract* he explicitly admitted that Rousseau's principle, though incontestable in theory, was inapplicable in practice in governments other than the purely democratic. Calonne was concerned to show that the methods by which representatives could be prevented from usurping power lay in other directions. Like many conservative writers he pinned his faith upon the mandate and argued that all the actions of the Assembly were illegal from the point at which the deputies had departed from the instructions contained in their *cahiers*: representatives were not the emissaries of that abstract entity 'the Nation', but delegates elected within a specific area, and responsible to their electors within that area.[1]

It is in relation to this argument that the conservative demand for ratification must be seen. Although these writers used the democratic language of the *Social Contract*, they did not intend to suggest that the laws should be subject to a national referendum and a majority vote. Rather they looked backward to the older concept of the Estates General, in which each deputy represented a specific section of the nation, each with its peculiar rights and historic liberties. In so far as rights and liberties had been swept aside and the legitimate claims of specific sections of the nation disregarded, the Assembly had acted despotically. The conservative insistence on ratification was not, therefore, simply a Rousseauist stick with which to beat the Assembly. In essence it represented the desperate gropings of the minority for a doctrine of defence against the totalitarianism of the majority. The revolutionaries had stated

[1] Calonne, *De l'état de France*, etc., 1790, p. 338.

that the law was the expression of the general will and valid only in so far as the nation willed it. The conservatives twisted this argument to their own use with urgent dexterity and claimed that the laws were not valid because they, as part of the nation, had neither willed them nor sanctioned them. They refused to accept that the laws were valid simply because one section of the nation had enforced them upon the other and smaller part. By means of the mandate, the minority could have been protected. Once, however, the mandate had been swept away, the principle of ratification could have only theoretical value for conservative writers, for they shrank from direct democracy, to which the practical application of this theory would have brought them. Thus they put forward no practical suggestions as to how the laws should be ratified by the nation, but they were none the less sincere in their resentment against laws which were imposed upon them by a majority and which they had neither sanctioned nor willed.

What, then, in the view of these writers, should the role of the Constituent Assembly have been? On this point they were less definite. One explanation was given by the author of the article *Sophismes politiques*. Since the deputies of the National Assembly had declared themselves legislators, he wrote, then they could not logically claim to exercise political power. According to the *Social Contract* the duty of the Assembly was to draw up a code of laws and present them to the nation. It could not, however, touch the ancient laws, and when its task was done, then the twelve hundred fractions of which the legislator had been composed should vanish before the nation like stars before the dawn. Neither this writer nor other conservative exponents of the Rousseauist concept of the legislator's role explained how the executive was to be prevailed upon to accept reforms emanating from a constituent assembly which, according to the conservative hypothesis, would presumably have been acting according to the mandates of its electors, and could therefore have been regarded as expressing the national will. This difficulty was, however, neatly resolved by Ferrand, also on Rousseauist principles. He quoted Rousseau's assertion that it was better that the government should abuse the laws than that the legislator should be corrupted by assuming the power to apply the laws as well as that of drawing them up.[1] Thus it would seem that in the last resort these writers were prepared to regard the King as the final arbiter of the nation's destinies, and to recognize in him the right which they denied to the Assembly, that of deciding what the laws should be and also of applying them. Like d'Antraigues, they regarded the representative assembly, and not the executive, as the most sinister threat to the liberty and well-being of the people.

In discussing the Rousseauist concept of the general will, aristocratic and conservative writers protested both against the revolutionary identification of the general will with the will of the majority, and against what they regarded as the claim of a despotic minority to express the general will of the nation. There is no fundamental cleavage between these two view-points. As shown above, the anti-revolutionaries accused the deputies in the Assembly of substituting their particular wills for the general will, and of misleading the ignorant mass of the nation.[2] The majority, it was claimed, were deceived by revolutionary orators and publicists, while honest citizens were prevented from expressing their opinions by every kind of pressure and even by coercion.

The nation had fallen prey, one writer asserted, to a seditious clique.[3] It was impossible, moreover, that the general will could be expressed as the result of long, tumultuous and acrimonious debates. It was precisely these conditions which Rousseau recognized as a sign that the general will was no longer in the ascendant, but that it had been eclipsed by particular wills.[4]

The general will was identified, in aristocratic pamphlets, with the rule of law, and the protection of the lives and property of the citizens, which the Assembly, it appeared, was either unwilling or unable to maintain. In such turbulent times it was not the general will which found expression, it was argued, but the will of a violent and vociferous minority. How, Lenormant asked, could an honest man state an opinion contrary to that

[1] Ferrand, *Adresse d'un citoyen*, etc., 1789, p. 26.

[2] See pp. 129–32 above.

[3] Anon., *La décadence de l'Empire français*, 1790, p. 5.

[4] Lenormant, *Rousseau, aristocrate*, 1790, pp. 52–3, 55. Malouet, *Opinion sur le projet de décret*, etc., 1790, p. 14. Anon., *Le dernier cri*, etc., 1791, p. 83.

of the multitude in tumultuous assemblies, without endangering his own life and fortune, and that of his family? 'Ce n'est pas dans un moment de crise et d'anarchie qu'on peut connaître l'expression de la volonté générale,' he wrote, 'Ce n'est pas au milieu du tumulte des passions, et des haînes particulières que la liberté peut régner. . . .' Moreover, he said, 'ce serait étrangement abuser des mots que de vouloir appliquer cette maxime à la formation de lois que la partie la plus nombreuse du peuple ne saurait comprendre; et Rousseau, qui a écrit cette maxime, était bien loin lui-même de vouloir en faire une pareille application.'[1]

Ferrand, examining Chapter III of Book II of the *Social Contract*, wrote that the character of the Assembly's decrees fully vindicated Rousseau's warnings. He wrote that he would have concluded that the Assembly did not will the good of society had not his attention been drawn, by the author of the *Social Contract*, to the possibility that the Assembly, although it might will the good, might not always be capable of perceiving it. This, he said, left him with the alternative of supposing that the Assembly was either ill-informed or ill-intentioned. As for the people, he disagreed with Rousseau's maxim that they may be mistaken, but never corrupted. They were certainly mistaken, he wrote, but they were also being corrupted, and particularly the people of Paris.[2]

Conservative writers had, however, a more positive contribution to make towards a definition of the general will, and this was probably closer to Rousseau's intentions than was revolutionary practice. In the first place the general will was equated with the transcendent rule of reason, unaffected by majorities or minorities. Clermont-Tonnerre, speaking of the transition of mankind to civil society, described the general will as follows: 'Les hommes éclairés sur les maux qu'entraîne ce désordre se réunissent en société, déclarent que leur volonté est que les individus se conforment aux notions naturelles du juste et de l'injuste. Cette volonté générale devient la loi. . . .'[3] Malouet wrote that reason existed in faithful submission to the general

[1] Lenormant, *Rousseau, aristocrate*, 1790, pp. 50–2.
[2] Ferrand, *Adresse d'un citoyen*, etc., 1790, pp. 8–9.
[3] Clermont-Tonnerre, *Sur la question du droit de guerre et de paix*, 1790, p. 3.

will, which always directed men toward liberty, justice and peace: 'La volonté générale est de sa nature simple et invariable: elle s'applique uniquement à la conservation, au bien être de chaque individu: elle a chez les Hottentots, non les même développements, mais le même caractère que parmi nous.'[1]

The underlying and constant interest of many of the conservative critics of the Assembly was, however, to oppose its claim to make any fundamental changes in French government. Thus many writers went beyond the position taken by Rousseau in the *Social Contract*. For example, some clearly regarded the monarchy as the personification of that rule of disinterested justice which they identified with the general will, and which alone they regarded as capable of regulating the whole community to its best advantage. It was claimed by some writers that it was the King who expressed the constant and general will of the nation, as opposed to the transient will of the deputies who, it was argued, were subject to particular interests and personal ambitions.[2] Rousseau's authority was explicitly used to support this argument.[3] Maury alone admitted that, according to Rousseau's principles, it was impossible for the general will to find expression at all in a large state.[4]

Conservative writers came closer to the concept of the general will, as it is developed in the *Social Contract*, in the emphasis which they placed upon the relationship between the laws and the moral habits and customs of the people. They echoed Rousseau's statement that the most important laws were those which were written on the heart, and they denied, on Rousseau's authority, that the establishment of a new constitution, even though it should be based on the most enlightened and rational principles, was capable of changing the character of a people. The laws themselves were not enough, they argued, to make a people good. They insisted that the laws must be related to those primary habits of virtue which Rousseau regarded as most important of all. Hence the ancient customs and

[1] Malouet, *Opinion sur le projet de décret*, etc., 1789, p. 12.

[2] D'Antraigues, *Sur la sanction royale*, 1789. Malouet, *Sur la sanction royale*, 1789. Bergasse, *Sur la manière de limiter le pouvoir législatif*, 1790.

[3] Anon., *Le Reveil des Rois*, 1791, p. 9.

[4] Maury, *Opinion sur le souveraineté*, etc., 1790, p. 125.

traditional laws were regarded as directed toward the good of the whole community and as embodying the general will, while the new laws were regarded as the products of error or ambition.

Finally, it is clear that in the minds of conservative writers the traditional customs were regarded as embodying, in the life of the nation, something of that transcendent rule of justice which they designated as Divine or natural law. For the minority to submit to the majority, they argued, it was necessary that there should be agreement on the fundamental conventions of society, and a common conviction of their justice.[1] What made will general, wrote one writer, echoing Rousseau, was not the number of voices, but the common interest which united men in a society where every individual submits to the same conditions that he imposes upon others. So long as counting heads was the only rule of justice, then the common rule of justice, which should unite those who judge with those who are judged, disappeared, and a collection of partial associations, such as Rousseau described in the *Social Contract*, took its place.[2]

Thus the anti-revolutionary writers appealed to a concept of traditional social values and the common standards of a transcendent justice in opposition to the revolutionary identification of the general will with the will of the majority. Indeed, from the point of view of the minority it is difficult to see how the will of the majority differs from the arbitrary will of a despot. Anti-revolutionary writers constantly protested about the despotism of the majority, whether expressed in the direct action of the people or in the decrees of the Assembly. They protested equally strongly, however, against the charge of despotism brought against the monarchy of the Ancien Régime. This was indeed understandable, for traditional privileges and liberties had to a large extent nullified the power of the monarchy to act despotically. With the abolition of these, however, those who had benefited from them were left unprotected before the reforming zeal of the Assembly.

[1] Ferrand, *Le dernier coup*, etc., 1790, p. 16. Anon., *Le Tableau de rapprochement*, 1790, p. 48.

[2] Anon., *Le Tableau de rapprochement*, 1790, p. 47.

It is interesting to note, however, that at least one anti-revolutionary writer found it difficult to retain his association of the idea of law as expressing universal reason and justice with a phrase which came increasingly to be identified by the revolutionaries with the popular will. In the speeches and writings of Malouet, who made frequent references to Rousseau, it is possible to trace this changing attitude to the expression 'la volonté générale', during 1789–91. In 1790, Malouet described the law as 'une intention juste et utile, exprimée par une volonté souveraine'; he used the expression 'the general will' to describe the rule of reason and natural law, stating that 'la volonté générale tend invariablement à la liberté, à la paix, et au bonheur de tous'. In 1791, however, he criticized Rousseau for having ever used the expression at all, since it was an anomalous phrase, bound to give rise to misunderstandings. Instead of identifying the general will with the rule of justice, he now distinguished between the general will, which, he said, may be unjust, and the law, which, he said, ought never to be.[1] Thus is appears that the phrase which Malouet originally identified with the rule of reason and justice had become closely associated in his mind with the idea of majority rule, and majority rule so odious to him that Malouet could no longer retain the concept of the general will as the expression of universal reason and justice within the context of his own political philosophy.

[1] Compare: *Motion sur le discours adressé par le roi à l'Assemblée Nationale*, 1789; *Lettre à ses commettans*, 1790; *Opinion sur l'acte constitutionnel*, 1791.

CHAPTER XI

The Defence of the Monarchy

CONSERVATIVE and royalist pamphleteers found the *Social Contract* valuable in their attack upon what they regarded as the reduction of the monarchy to a state of dependence upon, and subservience to, a popular assembly. They accused the revolutionaries of trying to establish in France that democratic and republican form of government which Rousseau regarded as possible only in small states. Rousseau had specified very particular conditions for the establishment of such a government, for he demanded not only that the state should be small enough for the citizens to know one another, but also that there should be a large measure of equality of fortune and simplicity of manners. How, these writers asked, could such conditions be regarded as applying to France? Rousseau had held that the form of government of any state must relate to the size of its population and the circumstances of its people, and he held monarchy to be the most appropriate form of government for large states.[1]

One pamphleteer drew attention to the extensive powers which Rousseau attributed to the monarchy in his *Considérations sur le gouvernement de Pologne*. These included the presidency of the diet and the senate and of all governing bodies, together with responsibility for the conduct of all officers, the dispensation of justice, the integrity of all tribunals, the maintenance of public order and the command of the army. These functions,

[1] Ferrand, *Adresse d'un citoyen*, etc., 1789, pp. 29–31. Anon., *L'Assemblée Nationale*, 1789, let. xvii, p. 225. Anon., *Lettre de J. J. Rousseau*, etc., 1789, p. 6. Lenormant, *Rousseau aristocrate*, 1790, pp. 31, 38 ff. Maury, *Opinion sur la souveraineté*, etc., 1790, pp. 27, 70–5. Anon., *Catéchisme anti-constitutionnel*, etc., 1790, p. 27. Anon., *Le Tableau de rapprochement*, 1790, p. 28. Anon., *La Monarchie vengée*, etc., 1791. p. 53. Anon., *Le Réveil des Rois*, etc., 1791, p. 11.

moreover, Rousseau had regarded as essential, not for an hereditary monarch such as the king of France, but for a king whose position was simply that of an elected chief.[1]

Again, it was claimed that according to Rousseau there could be no place for popular elections in the monarchical state, and his insistence on the right of the king to nominate all prelates and judges was emphasized.[2] It was pointed out that Rousseau described the institution of kingship as originating in the dispensation of justice; the king was the fountain of justice in the state and could not be divested of this primary function.[3]

Since, according to the *Social Contract*, intermediate bodies were essential to monarchy,[4] Rousseau's name was used to condemn the attack upon hereditary titles and the levelling of ranks. One pamphleteer, writing in 1789, argued that Rousseau's insistence on the need for intermediate bodies was the logical corollary of his concepts of monarchy and representation, because, if monarchy tended towards despotism, and if the sovereignty of the people was incapable of representation, then intermediate bodies were necessary to restrain the despotism of the prince on the one hand and the direct authority of the people on the other.[5] The majority of pamphleteers writing in 1790, however, were more interested in defending the position of intermediate bodies by reference to those disadvantages which Rousseau perceived in the institution of representation, than in relation to those which he attributed to monarchy. They pointed out that Rousseau held that the vices of 'aristocracy' were not confined necessarily to the patrician families but could also become characteristic of popular assemblies. It was argued, moreover, that the despotism of Paris was both a

[1] Anon., *Le dernier cri*, etc., 1791, p. 84.

[2] Clermont-Tonnerre, *Sur le droit que le monarque doit avoir*, etc., 1790, p. 5. Lenormant, *Rousseau, aristocrate*, 1790, pp. 41–2. Maury, *Sur le droit qui appartient aux Rois*, etc., 1790, p. 22.

[3] Anon., *Le dernier cri*, etc., 1791, p. 85.

[4] Anon., *L'Assemblée Nationale*, 1789, Let. xvii, p. 225. Anon., *Lettre de J. J. Rousseau*, etc., 1789, pp. 4, 5. Lenormant, *Rousseau, aristocrate*, 1790, p. 31. Anon., *L'Abus des mots*, 1790, p. 3. Anon., *Le Tableau de rapprochement*, 1790, p. 29. Anon., *Adresse à tous les membres*, etc., 1791, p. 12. Anon., *Le dernier cri*, etc., 1791, p. 85. Anon., *Le Réveil des Rois*, 1791, p. 18.

[5] Anon., *Le disciple de Montesquieu*, etc., 1789, p. 94.

cause and an effect of the new rule of equality.[1] One writer drew attention to Rousseau's praise for the Roman institution of client and patron,[2] and it was argued that in his own lifetime Rousseau held the noblesse in great respect and had a high esteem for many of its individual members.[3]

With justification it was observed that Rousseau's own concept of the powers of kingship far exceeded the claims which the most extreme royalists would dare to put forward to the National Assembly.[4] Nevertheless, Rousseau's views on monarchy were pushed to their extreme limit by the advocates of monarchical power. For example, Rousseau's name was used to support his argument that the National Assembly existed solely by the king's grace and that it had no independent powers or rights. Thus, in perpetuating its own existence and in enlarging its sphere of action and initiative beyond the recognized limits of the traditional Estates General, the Assembly had been guilty of a usurpation of power and an invasion of the royal prerogative.[5] The abbé Maury used Rousseau's definition of the contract to deny the right of the people to have any influence upon their form of government. According to Rousseau, he wrote, the contract is among the people themselves and not between the people and their leaders. No contract existed between the French people and the monarchy and therefore the former had no right to lay down terms to the latter. Maury argued that all great peoples had been formed by conquest and not by the people assembling to make contracts. He agreed with Rousseau that force did not make right, but he departed from him in maintaining that governments were justified not according to the principles of their origins, but according to their achievements and intentions. By this criterion he insisted that the French monarchy had justified its existence over many centuries. Moreover, he wrote, according to Rousseau every individual signified his acceptance of the form of the state by the simple fact of residence, so that although the monarchy originated in conquest, its legitimacy had long been established

[1] Anon., *Le Tableau de rapprochement*, 1790, p. 57, note 2.
[2] Ibid., p. 58, n. 1.
[3] Anon., *Lettre de J. J. Rousseau*, etc., 1789, p. 4.
[4] Lenormant, *Rousseau, aristocrate*, 1790, p. 15.
[5] Anon., *Lettre de J. J. Rousseau*, etc., 1789, p. 6.

by the beneficial character of its rule and by the acceptance of generations of the French people.[1] Both Maury and the anonymous author of the pamphlet *Le Réveil des Rois* denied that a nation could be said to have rights when in fact conditions precluded the possibility of their ever assembling to exercise them. The monarchy became in such circumstances the organ of the people's will and the interpreter of its intentions.[2]

On the basis of Rousseau's definitions of monarchy, the decrees of the National Assembly were examined and condemned. Rousseau, Lenormant asserted, was a disciple of Montesquieu, and as such would have deplored the invasion of the legislative power into the field of the executive. How, he asked, could Rousseau's concept of kingship be recognized in the King of France, whose co-operation was not necessary to make the laws, who could not command obedience from the administration unless his orders were confirmed by the Legislature, who could not make war and peace, and who could neither give his people judges nor refuse the investiture of one whom he knew to be undesirable?[3] Attention was drawn to Rousseau's description of the unity of purpose and action which characterized monarchical government[4]; of the French constitution, on the contrary, Ferrand remarked that it would be difficult to imagine a constitution 'dans laquelle une aussi grande quantité d'efforts produise une inaction aussi entière'.[5] Maury accused the revolutionaries of trying to establish a 'royal democracy', which was a contradiction in terms.[6] French government was neither a monarchy nor a democracy, wrote one pamphleteer, but a government without form or name.[7] What would Rousseau have said of this government which had all the disadvantages of a republic and lacked all the advantages of a monarchy?[8] It was a republican form of govern-

[1] Maury, *Opinion sur la souveraineté*, etc., 1790, pp. 75–6, 84.

[2] Anon., *Le Réveil des Rois*, 1791, pp. 6–9. Compare: Anon., *Le despotisme décreté par l'Assemblée Nationale*, 1790, pp. 13, 17.

[3] Lenormant, *Rousseau, aristocrate*, 1790, pp. 16–17. See also: Anon., *Le quatorze juillet*, etc., 1790, passim.

[4] Anon., *Le Tableau de rapprochement*, 1790, p. 28.

[5] Ferrand, *Adresse d'un citoyen*, etc., 1789, p. 30.

[6] Maury, *Opinion sur la souveraineté*, etc., 1790, p. 38.

[7] Anon., *Le Réveil des Rois*, 1791, pp. 17, 18.

[8] Anon., *Le Tableau de rapprochement*, 1790, p. 27.

ment in which the title of monarchy had been retained solely in order to deceive the nation.[1] This, however, another writer asserted, was a temporary measure only, for as soon as it was convenient then the monarchy would cease to exist and the republic would emerge as the true government.[2]

The possibility of such a transformation was, of course, denied. According to Rousseau only a people of gods could support democracy, and the French people could not even aspire to the more earthly virtues of the antique republics which Rousseau had so much admired.[3] Rousseau had approved of Plato's refusal to give laws to the Arcadians and Cyrenaeans,[4] for he was aware that laws cannot be imposed on a people; they must be rooted in tradition.[5] The French nation was not a *tabula rasa* on which the National Assembly could write what it pleased. It had been moulded for centuries by its monarchy and the French people could not shake off their past and change their characters with their laws.[6] Rousseau himself had described the effects of insurrection on a people who, thinking they were breaking the chains that bound them destroyed instead the very fabric of the state and plunged it into anarchy.[7] The Revolution, in fact, had sacrificed the monarchy and cast away the traditional virtues in order to pursue chimerical ideals to which the French people could never aspire.[8]

[1] Lenormant, *Rousseau, aristocrate*, 1790, p. 17 ff. Anon., *Le Tableau de rapprochement*, 1790, pp. 28, 41–2. Anon., *Le Réveil des Rois*, 1791, pp. 17–18.

[2] Lenormant, *Rousseau, aristocrate*, 1790, p. 18.

[3] Ibid., p. 24. See also: Ferrand, *Adresse d'un citoyen*, etc., 1789, p. 28. Anon., *Apologie de la noblesse*, etc., 1790, p. 58. Anon., *Catéchisme anti-constitutionnel*, 1790, p. 8. Anon., *Qui est-ce donc qui gagne?*, etc., 1790, p. 24. Anon., *Adresse à tous les membres*, etc., 1791, p. 10. Anon., *Le dernier cri*, etc., 1791, p. 86. Anon., *La Monarchie vengée*, etc., 1791, p. 52. Anon., *Le Réveil des Rois*, 1791, pp. 31–2. Anon., *Les Sabats Jacobites*, No. XIII, 1791, title page.

[4] Anon., *Catéchisme anti-constitutionnel*, 1790, p. 5. Anon., *Le Réveil des Rois*, 1791, p. 31.

[5] Anon., *Catéchisme anti-constitutionnel*, 1790, p. 6.

[6] Anon., *Lisez ceci bons Français*, 1790, p. 2. See also Anon., *Le Réveil des Rois*, 1791, p. 33.

[7] Ferrand, *Adresse d'un citoyen*, etc., 1789, p. 41. Montlosier, *L'Art de constituer les peuples*, 1790, pp. 18–19. Anon., *La décadence de l'Empire Français*, 1790, p. 18. Anon., *Qui est-ce donc qui gagne?*, etc., 1790, pp. 24–5. Anon., *Le Réveil des Rois*, 1791, pp. 33–4. Anon., *Les Sabats Jacobites*, No. IV, 1791, title page.

[8] Anon., *Catéchisme anti-constitutionnel*, 1790, p. 33. Anon., *La décadence de l'Empire Français*, 1790, p. 7. Anon., *Le Tableau de rapprochement*, 1790, p. 39. Anon., *Le Réveil des Rois*, 1791, p. 33.

Can the monarchists be regarded as interpreting Rousseau's theories fairly, or were they, as they accused their political opponents of being, purely opportunist in their utilization of Rousseau's ideas? It has already been shown that the conservative exposition of Rousseau's theory was more exact and more closely related to Rousseau's texts than the interpretations of the revolutionaries. The conservatives could support their arguments by reference to Rousseau's works without drastic misinterpretation of his theories more easily than their opponents were able to do. But they were also able to make good use of the duality of Rousseau's theory and this sometimes gives an appearance of sophistry to their arguments. For example, on the one hand they criticized the intentions and achievements of the revolutionaries in relation to the ideal principles stated by Rousseau in the *Social Contract*; on the other hand they were able to support the traditional institutions of the Ancien Régime on the ground of the inevitability of certain forms of social and political organization for certain types of society, as maintained by the same author in the *Social Contract*, the *Considérations sur le gouvernement de Pologne*, and in the comments to the two works of the abbé de Saint-Pierre. Thus, while the National Assembly was condemned in the light of Rousseau's abstract principles of political justice, the monarchy was justified by that alternative set of principles supplied by the author of the *Social Contract*, the principles of historical and political necessity which, in Rousseau's view, demanded that large states should be ruled by the monarchical form of government.

Moreover, while distinguishing between Rousseau's ideals and his recognition of the necessity, in practice, of monarchy for large states, the anti-revolutionaries gave to his definition of the monarchical system the same ideal and emotional colouring as the revolutionaries gave to the concept of popular sovereignty. Rousseau's description of monarchy in the *Social Contract* was sometimes referred to and quoted as though Rousseau had been painting an ideal picture of this institution, rather than describing the inevitable but unfortunate fate of large nations. Moreover, since the monarchy and the National Assembly were judged according to different standards, criticisms which could be levelled against the Assembly were not regarded as capable of being justifiably levelled against the monarchy. For example, the deputies were constantly criticized on the basis of Rousseau's principle of the inalienability of sovereignty and blamed for having rejected their mandates. On the other hand, no reference was made to Rousseau's equally definite condemnation of monarchy, in the same work, as tending always toward despotism by precisely this process of the subjection of the general will to a particular will.

The distinction between the standards which could properly be applied to the monarchy and to the National Assembly is most clearly illustrated in the arguments dealing with the separation of powers in the branches of government, and in the view taken by conservative writers as to how power should be allocated between the executive and legislative branches of the government. While, on Rousseau's authority, the powers of the constituent assembly were narrowly limited and strictly defined in the arguments of those writers, the powers of the executive, also on Rousseau's authority, were given the widest possible interpretation. The right of the executive to nominate the judges was warmly defended, but the action of the Assembly in divesting the King of this power and placing it in the hands of a representative assembly was attacked as an offence against the principle of the separation of powers. Again, it was denied that the Assembly could claim the power both to draw up the laws and to establish them, a denial which, had it been applied, would have nullified the possibility of effective action on the part of the Assembly. Such a view of the functions of the Constituent Assembly presupposed the acceptance on its part of the executive as sole arbiter of the laws and sole judge of which reforms should be accepted and which rejected. Thus the monarchy was attributed in effect with the powers of legislation which, on Rousseau's authority, were denied to the Assembly.

It is true that these critics of the Assembly insisted that, according to Rousseau, ratification was necessary before any law could become valid. No proposals were made, however, for any machinery by which such ratification could be obtained. Once the first two orders had been deprived of the power of veto, the demand for ratification could hardly be regarded from a practical point of view as more than a useful controversial weapon, drawn from the *Social Contract*, with which to embarrass the Assembly. While these writers urged the necessity of ratification for the decrees of the Constituent Assembly, where the monarchy was concerned they fell back upon the assertion made by Rousseau in the *Social Contract* that in certain circumstances silence must be taken to mean consent.

These arguments were based on the traditional concepts of monarchical power. In the first place, when they discussed the division of powers, most of them understood by this term not the constitutional concept of a balance of powers, but rather the mutual independence of the two main branches of government. The monarchy was regarded as divinely ordained, or as deriving its authority from its historic role, and therefore as not being subject to the sanction of its citizens. Alternatively, it was described as deriving its power direct from the nation, as the permanently appointed chief representative of the people and the embodiment of the people's will, and therefore not accountable to a legislative assembly. Both these arguments were, of course, equally fatal to the idea of a representative assembly claiming the power to make and to establish the laws, and to supervise their execution in the name of the people. The conservatives and monarchists retained an ideal picture of the monarchy as above all human passions, disinterested, and acting always for the common good. In their predilection for the old order, they attributed to the traditional government the characteristics of the rule of justice and reason, while to that of the National Assembly they attributed all the vices of the rule of passion, personal ambitions and particular interests.

Nevertheless, in spite of conservative prejudices and the sophistries inevitable to political controversy, it is possible to maintain not only that the anti-revolutionary interpretations of Rousseau's political theory were both more detailed and more accurate than those of the revolutionaries, but also that their interpretations expressed Rousseau's real intentions much more closely than the revolutionaries could do. As these conservative Rousseauists themselves constantly pointed out, Rousseau did not regard his ideal principles as capable of realization except in rare circumstances. Moreover, while he could not accept the compromise of a representative system in any conditions, unless the deputies were denied the right and deprived of the opportunity to act on their own initiative, he was prepared to accept the necessity, and even it appears in some circumstances the advantages, of the power of a king. The anti-revolutionaries were hostile neither to Rousseau's memory nor to his political theory. Even those who rejected the fundamental doctrine of the sovereignty of the people were not prevented from eulogizing Rousseau and his works or from using the *Social Contract* to prove their points against their enemies. It was the later evaluation and propagation by the revolutionary cult of Rousseau's political theory which gave rise to the legend 'C'est la faute à Rousseau'. In 1789–91 this legend was not accepted by anti-revolutionary opinion. The facility with which Rousseau's political theory was adapted, without appreciable distortion, to the anti-revolutionary case was in itself sufficient reason for the aristocratic protest against the association of Rousseau's memory and works with the Revolution, and sufficient proof of the attitude of these writers to Rousseau's political theory.

PART IV

Conclusion

CHAPTER XII

The Revolutionary Cult of Rousseau

IN the first part of this work an attempt was made to show that the influence of Rousseau's political theories was by no means a major factor in the history of the first three years of the Revolution. It would appear that the *Social Contract* was not widely read either before 1789, or between 1789 and 1791. The majority of speakers and writers who appealed to the authority of Rousseau did so in order to put forward not Rousseau's views but their own, with the result that his name was frequently associated with arguments which were in direct contradiction with those which he had formulated. It is not unusual to find that when revolutionary writers actually studied the *Social Contract* they were critical of some aspects of Rousseau's political theory, particularly his condemnation of representation. It has been shown that the most careful analysis of Rousseau's political theory is to be found not in the pamphlets of revolutionary writers, but in those of the aristocratic critics of the Revolution who protested against the use of Rousseau's name to justify the deeds of the revolutionaries.

These conclusions, however, raise an important question. If it is denied that the political theory of Rousseau was well known to the men who played leading roles in the successive acts of the Revolution, how is it possible to explain the stubborn persistence of the revolutionary cult of Rousseau? How can the importance attached to Rousseau's name, and the homage paid to his memory from 1789 onward be reconciled with the apparent ignorance, or where it was not ignored, the misinterpretation, of his political theories?

No one would deny the ardour, enthusiasm and spontaneity with which the Revolution honoured Rousseau's memory in public demonstrations and official ceremonies, nor the constant association of his name with its achievements.[1] I do not propose here to describe in detail all the manifestations of the cult of Rousseau, but these must be referred to briefly. Rousseau's name was associated with the Revolution from a very early date. According to Girardin, when the news of the fall of the Bastille reached Mans, where he was garrisoned at the time, the citizens offered him the 'cocarde nationale', acclaiming him: 'Élève de Jean-Jacques, ton patriotisme te rend digne de la porter!'[2] Whether or not this account is true, it is certainly the case that Rousseau's name was associated with the victory of liberty and equality symbolized by the fall of the Bastille.[3] A bust was sculptured in stone taken from the Bastille, with the words '*Liberté*, *Égalité*, *Fraternité*' inscribed at its base, and on subsequent celebrations of the 14th July, a bust of Rousseau was carried in procession round the ruins of the fortress.[4]

A bust of Rousseau was also installed in the National Assembly in 1790, with copies of *Émile* and the *Social Contract* deposited at its base.[5] The Assembly accepted the presentation of the complete works of Rousseau in 1791.[6] Rousseau's bust was similarly installed in the assembly rooms of many popular societies between 1790 and 1791, including the Jacobins,[7] the *Société des Indigens*,[8] and the *Société du Cercle Social des Amis de la Vérité*.[9] Busts of Rousseau and quotations from his works decorated the *Autels de la Patrie*,[10], a section of Paris was named

[1] A detailed account of the Revolutionary cult of Rousseau is given by Gordon McNeil in 'The Cult of Rousseau and the French Revolution', *Journal of the History of Ideas*, April 1945, VI, No. 2.

[2] Girardin, *Discours et Opinions*, *Journal et Souvenirs*, 1828, pp. 69, 129.

[3] See Ginguené, *Lettres sur les Confessions de J. J. Rousseau*, 1791, p. 3.

[4] Aulard, *La Société des Jacobins*, I, 288.

[5] *Recueil des pièces relatives à la motion faite à l'Assemblée Nationale au sujet de J. J. Rousseau et de sa veuve*, Paris, 1791. The copies of these two works were presented by d'Eymar, who proposed the motion.

[6] See Tuetey, *Répertoire général*, etc., 1890–1912, II, No. 3569, 14 April 1791. The publisher Poincot made this presentation.

[7] See Aulard, *Société des Jacobins*, III, 219.

[8] Vachard, *Installation de J. J. Rousseau . . . dans la Société des Indigens*, etc., 1791. See also Tourneux, *Bibliographie de Paris*, etc., 1890–1906, II, No. 9900.

[9] *Bouche de Fer*, December 1790, No. 36, pp. 547–53; 6 January 1791, No. 2, p. 20; 13 January 1791, No. 5, pp. 65–6.

[10] See Mathiez, *Les Origines des cultes révolutionnaires*, 1904, p. 88.

'*Contrat Social*',[1] and a street in Paris received his name in 1791.[2]

Fêtes were held in Rousseau's honour, the most famous of which was that held at Montmorency in September 1791.[3] As early as 1789 a fête was celebrated in Angers in honour of Rousseau and Voltaire.[4] Hymns and poems to Rousseau were a frequent feature in revolutionary and literary journals, and invocations to his name were regularly made by orators and pamphleteers. A number of plays on the subject of Rousseau's life enjoyed considerable success in Paris. One such play, performed in 1791, was particularly popular. It depicted the last days of Rousseau, spent in modest retirement, and his death. Protests, however, were aroused by the author's introduction of the character of the Marquis de Girardin into the death-bed scene, since some members of the audience regarded it as unseemly that an aristocrat should be depicted as present at the sacred moment.[5]

Before the National Assembly officially decreed a statue to Rousseau in December 1790, a number of private projects for this purpose had been set on foot. The journal *Révolutions de Paris* opened a fund for the erection of a statue to Rousseau under the inspiration of Sylvain Maréchal.[6] Finally, in November and December 1790, Rousseau's name was officially honoured by the state. The National Assembly decreed the erection of a statue in his honour, and granted a pension to his widow.[7] In August of the following year the Assembly received

[1] Tuetey, *Répertoire général*, etc., II, No. 2625, 4 May 1791.

[2] Ibid. 1 June 1791.

[3] See *Fête champêtre célébrée à Montmorency en l'honneur de J. J. Rousseau*, 1791.

[4] See Proust, *Le triomphe de la philosophie*, etc., 1789.

[5] The play was entitled *Les derniers moments de J. J. Rousseau*, and was performed at the Théâtre des Italiens in 1790.

[6] *Révolutions de Paris*, 23–30 January 1790, No. 29, p. 44. Lists of subscribers were published in subsequent editions. In the issue of 27 November–4 December 1790, No. 73, p. 423, it was pointed out that although the fund had been open almost a year, the amount collected amounted only to 2,585 livres; support had not been forthcoming from the Paris Clubs. In December, as a result of the official honours paid to Rousseau's memory by the National Assembly, the project was abandoned. The money was used for the aid of children whose parents were killed during the siege of the Bastille. See 15–22 January 1791, No. 80, p. 91.

[7] *Recueil des pièces relatives à la motion faite à l'Assemblée au sujet de J. J. Rousseau et de sa veuve*, 1790.

two petitions demanding the transference of Rousseau's remains from Ermenonville to the Panthéon. The first of these, instigated by Ginguené, who also introduced a motion on the same subject in the National Assembly, was supported by a large number of well known admirers of Rousseau.[1] The second petition was presented by the citizens of Montmorency.[2] It has been suggested that it was the opposition of Girardin which prevented the removal of the remains of Rousseau to the Panthéon in 1791. There is, however, some evidence that opposition was more widely spread. The sentimental association of Rousseau's memory with the Île des Peupliers was too strong to be effaced without opposition in a generation which had made pilgrimages to that romantic spot and indulged in all the excesses of *sensibilité* over Rousseau's tomb. It was argued that the solitude and beauty of Ermenonville made a more suitable resting place for the friend of nature than the Panthéon.[3] It was not until 1794, when Voltaire's remains had already been transferred to the Panthéon, that this final honour was paid to Rousseau.

The honours paid to Rousseau's memory during the Revolution have been regarded by historians as evidence of the influence exercised by his political theory. This is a patent *non sequitur*. In order to discover the precise nature of the cult of Rousseau, and its roots in the revolutionary mind, it is necessary to examine not simply the outward manifestations of the cult, such as those which have been described above, but also the ideas which emerged in relation to it, and the particular concepts which were associated with Rousseau's name. How far, in fact, was the cult political and attributable to the influence of the *Social Contract*?

Certain general ideas were associated with the Rousseauist cult. Rousseau was hailed as the founder of the constitution on

[1] *Pétition à l'Assemblée Nationale*, etc., 1791. This petition was drawn up by Ginguené.

[2] *Pétition des citoyens de la ville et du canton de Montmorency à l'Assemblée Nationale*, 1791.

[3] See, for example, *Révolutions de Paris*, 27 August–3 September 1791, No. 112, p. 365 ff. and 3–10 September 1791, No. 113. In the latter was published the letter from Girardin to the National Assembly, opposing transference of Rousseau's remains from Ermenonville to the Panthéon. See p. 583 ff.

the ground that he had revealed to humanity the fundamental principles of justice and right which the revolutionaries claimed to be putting into effect. These were: the sovereignty of the people, liberty and equality. D'Eymar, in a speech in the National Assembly, proposing the erection of a statue to Rousseau, asserted:

> Vous verriez dans Jean-Jacques Rousseau . . . le précurseur de cette grande Révolution; vous vous souviendriez qu'il vous apprenait à former des hommes pour la liberté, lorsque vous étiez à la veille de faire des Français un peuple libre. . . . Le Contrat Social a été pour vous la charte dans laquelle vous avez retrouvé les droits usurpés sur la nation, et surtout le droit impréscriptible de souveraineté.[1]

Ginguené admitted that in some details the revolutionaries were not in fact following Rousseau's theories, but this, he said, did not in any way affect Rousseau's title to be considered as the father of the constitution:

> De quelle souveraineté fûtes-vous investis pour régénérer un grand empire, pour lui donner une constitution libre? De l'inaliénable et impréscriptible souveraineté du peuple. Sur quelle base avez-vous fondé cette constitution, qui deviendra le modèle de toutes les constitutions humaines? Sur l'égalité des droits. Or, Messieurs, l'égalité des droits entre les hommes et la souveraineté du peuple, Rousseau fut le premier à les établir en système, sous les yeux même du despotisme.[2]

Ginguené therefore concluded that Rousseau was the first founder of the constitution.

Other writers and orators made the same claims on Rousseau's behalf. The citizens of Montmorency called Rousseau 'ce vengeur indomptable des droits de l'homme', who had shown the means whereby societies could be recalled to their true purpose.[3] An anonymous pamphleteer, demanding the erection of a statue to Rousseau asserted: 'C'est parce que sur les points essentiels . . . il a vu et publié le premier la vérité . . . c'est que si la révolution actuelle est un grand bien, elle est son

[1] *Recueil des pièces*, etc. See *Motion relative à J. J. Rousseau*, by A. M. d'Eymar, 29 Dec. 1790, p. 7.

[2] *Pétition à l'Assemblée Nationale*, etc., 1791, pp. 2–3.

[3] *Pétition des citoyens . . . de Montmorency*, etc., 1791, p. 10.

ouvrage.'[1] The President of the National Assembly, replying to the petitions for the transference of Rousseau's remains to the Panthéon referred to him as the philosopher who had restored to men their equality of rights and to peoples their sovereignty. More important, he had prepared in men's hearts the love of liberty.[2] Collot d'Herbois, speaking in the Jacobin Club, hailed Rousseau as the patron of all peoples who loved liberty.[3] One writer designated him 'the father of liberty'.[4] At Montmorency the following inscription was carved on the base of the statue erected to Rousseau in 1791:

> Philosophe doux et modeste,
> Il a connu les droits de l'humanité,
> C'est dans cette vallée
> En contemplant l'ouvrage de la Divinité,
> Il a fait son Contrat Social
> La base de notre constitution.[5]

The significance of these and many more invocations to Rousseau must not be misinterpreted. When he was termed the founder of the constitution it was not in the sense that he had provided a kind of political and constitutional blue-print, but in the sense that he had formulated those basic principles of justice and those human rights which the makers of the constitution sought to guarantee. Why were these general principles ascribed to Rousseau? They cannot be regarded as peculiar to his political thought. The ideas of liberty, equality and the sovereignty of the people were general concepts accepted by the majority of those who supported the Revolution, and even by some who opposed it. They were not culled from the works of any one particular writer but belonged to that general body of eighteenth-century political theory to which not only the great philosophers but also the plagiarists and pamphleteers of the revolutionary and immediately pre-revolutionary period had contributed. The real problem therefore is why such widely

[1] Anon., *De J. J. Rousseau*, etc., 1790.

[2] *Réponse de M. le Président de l'Assemblée nationale*, etc., 1791. Broglie's reply, rejecting the proposal, was published with the two petitions.

[3] See *Journal des Jacobins*, 8 December 1791, No. 108.

[4] Vachard, *Installation de J. J. Rousseau*, etc., 1791, p. 1.

[5] See *Fête champêtre célébrée à Montmorency*, etc., 1791.

accepted ideas were associated particularly with Rousseau. It is of course true that his name was frequently used in conjunction with those of Voltaire, Montesquieu, Raynal, Mably and others. Nevertheless, the revolutionaries gave official recognition to Rousseau as a prophet and patron of the Revolution before they accorded the same recognition to any other philosopher. It is probably fair to say that more than that of any of the great pre-revolutionary writers, the memory of Rousseau captured the imagination of the revolutionary generation. It is in this last assertion that the true explanation of the Rousseauist cult will be found.

In order to understand the reasons why it was predominantly upon the name of Rousseau that these general revolutionary principles were fathered, it is necessary to take into account the fact that a cult of Rousseau already existed before the Revolution began, and that his name was already highly charged with ideas and emotions which, if not directly political, were nevertheless in a sense revolutionary. This cult the Revolution took over, but its transfiguration from a purely personal and literary to a political cult was possible only because the basic ideas which had been associated with Rousseau's name during the latter part of his life and after his death were as relevant to the revolutionaries as they had been to the preceding generation.

The pre-revolutionary cult of Rousseau had nothing to do with Rousseau's political theory, nor, except indirectly, with any political ideas. It was a personal and literary cult which owed its existence to the appeal of the *Nouvelle Héloise* and the *Émile* but even more to the personal legend of Rousseau. In this legend he featured as a captivating genius, a man of charm and gentleness, whose sufferings had not prevented him from laying down those sublime truths which he had learned in solitary communion with Nature, nor from being hounded by a perverse authority and betrayed by false friends. Seen through the eyes of that *sensibilité* of which he was the greatest eighteenth-century exponent, Rousseau's own person appeared larger than life; he became for his admirers the prototype of the natural and virtuous man whose education he had planned in *Émile*, and a living exemplar of the complex humanity which he had described in the *Nouvelle Héloise*, and later in his own

Confessions, and with which his readers could so easily identify themselves. Mornet has examined in detail the influence of the Rousseauist myth, both during Rousseau's own life-time and after his death, on the manners and attitudes of mind of his contemporaries and of the generation which followed.[1] In the works of Mornet, and in those of Buffenoir,[2] and Girardin[3] may be found many examples of the emotional ardour, and, after Rousseau's death, the religious fervour, which characterized the Rousseauist cult. Admirers of Rousseau visited him in a spirit of reverence, and later adherents of the Rousseauist cult made solemn pilgrimages to his tomb. The Prince de Ligne, describing his first visit to Rousseau, wrote:

> Despite my wishes I set the limit myself, and after a reverent silence spent gazing into the eyes of the author of the Nouvelle Héloise, I left that hovel, which was the home of rats, and at the same time the sanctuary of genius.[4]

The abbé Brizzard recorded his visits to Rousseau with exaggerated enthusiasm:

> I have seen him; I have conversed with the wisest of men. He accepted my youth, and I never left one of his conversations without feeling my soul uplifted and my heart more virtuous.[5]

After Rousseau's death, his tomb on the Île des Peupliers at Ermenonville took on the character of a national shrine, attracting many hundreds of pilgrims.[6] For the better preparation of their minds in approaching this hallowed spot the Marquis de Girardin addressed the visitors in a guide book to the grounds of Ermenonville:

> It is to you, friend of Rousseau, it is to you that I address myself; you alone are able to sense the affecting charm of such a site. In these solitary places, nothing can distract you from the object of

[1] See *Rousseau, l'homme et l'œuvre*, 1950, ch. iv; also *La pensée française au XVIII*[e] *siècle*, 1926, and Introduction to the *Nouvelle Héloise*, ed. Mornet, 1925, I, part IV, ch. I.

[2] See *Le prestige de J. J. Rousseau*, Paris, 1909, and *Les portraits de J. J. Rousseau*, 1913.

[3] See *Iconographie de J. J. Rousseau*, 1905.

[4] *Letters and Memoirs of the Prince de Ligne*, ed. Ashton, 1927, p. 158.

[5] G. Brizzard, *Socrate et Jean-Jacques*, etc. (n.d.).

[6] See Metra, *Correspondance secrète*, etc., 1789.

your love; you see it; it is there, let your tears pour out; never will you have wept sweeter or more justifiable tears.[1]

The most remarkable account of a pilgrimage to Rousseau's tomb is that given by the abbé Brizzard, who visited Ermenonville with a party of friends, all enthusiastic admirers of Rousseau. They first fell on their knees and kissed the tomb, after which each member of the party paid tribute to Rousseau's memory and laid flowers on the monument. Finally they tore out and burned ceremoniously those pages of Diderot's *Essai sur Sénèque* in which the author had attacked Rousseau. Brizzard described the sombreness of their surroundings as giving an impressively august setting to the scene which they enacted.[2]

It was this moral and personal cult which the Revolution appropriated. Professor McNeil, in his study of the revolutionary cult of Rousseau, takes the view that the revolutionary adoption of the Rousseauist cult involved a certain dissociation of the cult from the mainsprings of its origins so that it became to some extent artificial in its revolutionary context. He writes: 'There was practically none of the intensely personal and emotional loyalty to the "bon Jean-Jacques" that there was in the literary cult'. He concludes, moreover, that, 'as an expression of first this, and then that faction, the political cult could never achieve an independent existence or a rationale of its own.'[3]

A study of the ideas which emerged in relation to the Rousseauist cult during the Revolution makes it difficult, however, to accept these conclusions. In the first place it is difficult to see why the revolutionaries should have continued to pay homage to Rousseau's memory unless it were generally felt that the ideas which had been associated with his name before the

[1] Girardin, *Promenade ou Itinéraire des Jardins d'Ermenonville*, 1788, p. 24. Quoted by McNeil, *The Cult of Rousseau*, etc., p. 200.

[2] G. Brizzard, *Pélerinage à Ermenonville aux mânes de J. J. Rousseau*, 1783. An account of a more restrained, but probably more typical, visit to Ermenonville is given by Mme. Roland. She and her father, accompanied by M. de Boismorel, wandered about the grounds of the park, or rested in the shade of the trees, where M. de Boismorel read to them from the works of Montesquieu. See *Vie Privée*, *Œuvres*, I, 231, 232. One visitor came to Ermenonville to commit suicide at the tomb in order that he might be buried near Rousseau. See McNeil, *The Cult of Rousseau*, etc., p. 202.

[3] McNeil, *The cult of Rousseau*, etc., p. 202.

Revolution were also relevant to revolutionary aspirations. The aristocrats, of course, accused the revolutionaries of using Rousseau's name simply as a cloak to give respectability to what they regarded as nefarious schemes, and it is certainly true that there was more than an element of expediency in the way in which revolutionary orators and writers appealed to Rousseau's authority. It would be a mistake, however, to explain the revolutionary cult simply in terms of opportunism. The pre-revolutionary and the revolutionary cult had a common rationale in the basic and fundamental idea of the moral regeneration of mankind. Rousseau had addressed himself to the individual; he had however stipulated that while men were potentially virtuous, society was immoral and corrupt. The revolutionaries had accepted the view that the regeneration of the individual could be brought about by the regeneration of society; and because it was with the name of Rousseau that the idea of individual moral regeneration had become particularly associated, so, in carrying the idea into the wider sphere of social regeneration, it was with Rousseau's name that the practical devices of the Revolution were associated. Since Rousseau had stated the ends, then the means adopted by the Revolution were also regarded as having been approved by Rousseau. Moreover since Rousseau's political principles had been set forth in the *Social Contract*, then this work had to be made to conform to the preconceived notions as to its contents. Thus, while the general political ideas which were grafted on to the Rousseauist cult had little or nothing to do with the theories put forward by Rousseau in the *Social Contract*, they had a great deal to do with that concept of Rousseau as a great moral teacher which was common both to the pre-revolutionary and the revolutionary Rousseauist cult.

This basic concept of Rousseau's moral role emerges continuously and emphatically in revolutionary writings.

'Ce qui plaça J. J. Rousseau au-dessus de tous les écrivains de son siècle,' wrote Mercier, 'c'est que son éloquence avait un caractère moral.'[1] More than any other writer Rousseau's name was associated with the idea of social regeneration.[2] He was

[1] Mercier, p. 19.

[2] See Champion, *Rousseau et la Révolution française*, ch. xx, 'Le feu sacré'.

indeed regarded as having laid the necessary foundations of the Revolution by rescuing the individual from the toils of corruption and recalling him to the path of virtue. He was considered to have prepared the way for the social regeneration which the revolutionaries believed they were bringing about, by teaching the need for individual moral regeneration. D'Escherny claimed that Rousseau's *First* and *Second Discourses* had inaugurated a new examination of the moral nature of man as the basis of a new science of society.[1] Rousseau's authority was invoked to plead for the alliance of public and private morality as the prerequisite of a regenerated state.[2] Aubert de Vitry wrote an imaginary conversation between the spirits of the great philosophers of the eighteenth century on the subject of the Revolution. He gave Rousseau a leading role in this discussion, because it was Rousseau who in his view had initiated that *restauration des mœurs* which had been the necessary prelude to the Revolution. He is made to say:

. . . ce sont mes écrits; qui ayant d'abord opéré une révolution dans la vie privée, finiront par en opérer également une dans la vie publique.[3]

The same aspects of Rousseau's role were emphasized in various official pronouncements. D'Eymar argued that the National Assembly was only completing the work of regeneration which Rousseau had begun.[4] Ginguené claimed that Rousseau had rescued the people from frivolity and false conventions, and that he had brought about the moral regeneration without which their own attempts to bring about a regeneration of the laws would have been fruitless.[5] On the *autel de la patrie* at Rennes, Rousseau's own words were inscribed:

La patrie ne peut subsister sans la liberté; la liberté sans la vertu.[6]

It is not therefore possible to accept the view that the revolutionary cult of Rousseau lacked a rationale of its own. On

[1] D'Escherny, *Éloge de J. J. Rousseau*, etc., 1790.
[2] See the discussion of *Révolutions de Paris*, in Ch. XI.
[3] See the Introduction to Aubert de Vitry, *J. J. Rousseau à l'Assemblée nationale*, 1789.
[4] *Motion relative à J. J. Rousseau*, etc., p. 7.
[5] *Pétition à l'Assemblée nationale*, etc., 1791, p. 3.
[6] Mathiez, *Les Origines des cultes*, etc., p. 40.

the contrary, the personal legend of Rousseau acquired a new significance as a result of the Revolution. Rousseau became the symbol of the virtuous man who suffers at the hands of tyranny, pride and privilege, but who courageously fights back with the weapons of truth. The revolutionaries regarded Rousseau as their forerunner. Saint-Just, discussing the characteristics of the 'revolutionary man', and reciting his innumerable virtues, concluded by asserting that Rousseau was the type of man he was describing.[1] In an article in the *Bouche de Fer*, a writer described the 'Caractère de ces hommes rares destinés par la nature, comme Jean-Jacques, à réveiller les nations'. Such a man, the writer asserted, is destined by nature to suffer, but never to lose his love of humanity; to be surrounded by deceitfulness, but never to lose sight of truth. His struggle is that of a god of nature against the demons of tyranny. 'Pauvre Jean-Jacques, tu as fourni les traits de l'homme extraordinaire et toujours méconnu, qui doit influer sur les destins de l'univers. Il a souffert pour la liberté, combattu pour la liberté, il vient de conquérir la divine liberté!'[2]

Writing after the Revolution, Étienne Dumont pointed out that Rousseau's influence was especially strong amongst the bourgeoisie, because those who were discontented with their social status, or who suffered under the system of privilege and corruption which Rousseau attacked could identify themselves in Rousseau's 'martyrdom'. They embraced him as an 'avenger', a 'tribune of the people and of virtue'. As Dumont recognized, however, Rousseau's appeal was not confined to any one section of the community. It was universal, because the main content of his writing was his moral message, his recall to simple natural virtue.[3]

The idea of Rousseau as a great moral teacher assumed new significance as a result of the Revolution. It is not the case that the revolutionary cult did not give rise to the same 'intensely personal and emotional loyalty' which characterized the pre-revolutionary cult. On the contrary, Rousseau's memory excited the same religious fervour which was common to the

[1] *Œuvres complètes*, II, 372.
[2] *Bouche de Fer*, 28 February 1791, No. XXV.
[3] See 'Pages oubliées et inédites etc.', *Annales*, XXII (1933).

pre-revolutionary expressions of loyalty to his name. Again and again in revolutionary pamphlets the reader comes upon the highly emotional concept of Rousseau as a kind of Messiah who was persecuted, misunderstood and martyred, but whose theories were now, for the first time, being realized by his revolutionary disciples. Writers and speakers invoked the spirit of Rousseau and called upon him to look down and bless their undertakings; they pictured themselves as carrying out their master's injunctions beneath his benevolent eyes, and congratulated themselves on finally bringing peace and satisfaction to the spirit of one who had suffered persecution and death in order that they might find liberty.

An example of this almost religious fervour is to be found in an account of the installation of the bust of Rousseau at the *Société des Indigens*, in 1791. The writer concluded his description of the ceremony with a passionately expressed eulogy of Rousseau. He prayed to the spirit of Rousseau, who, he asserted, could read their hearts and minds, and asked him to return amongst them, to guide their footsteps. He referred to Rousseau as the instrument of God, who had helped humanity to gain their liberty at the cost of his own life. Finally, in a delirious outburst, he announced that Rousseau had heard their prayer, and had returned to guide them to their goal.

An account of a visit of a party of young Rousseauist enthusiasts to Ermenonville, as extravagant as any description of the pre-revolutionary pilgrimages to Rousseau's tomb, can be found in a pamphlet which was published in 1791. This describes how, on the evening of the 31st December of 1790, a society of friends of the 'citoyen philosophe' were assembled to discuss ways and means of defeating aristocratic plots against the constitution, when one of their members rushed in with the news of the Assembly's decree honouring Rousseau's memory. On this subject the new arrival made a lengthy and apparently extempore speech, after which it was decided that the occasion should be celebrated by a visit to Ermenonville. It was proposed to carve the Assembly's decree upon stone and offer it at Rousseau's tomb as a 'sacrifice' to his 'fiery spirit'. Six representatives were accordingly elected from their numbers and on the following day they set out for Ermenonville.

The author describes with much feeling their approach to the tomb, and how, as they drew near to the Île des Peupliers, they appeared to have entered a new spiritual world. They had an overpowering sense of the personality of Rousseau brooding over the spot, and of a supernatural peace which Nature herself forbade them to disturb. In this profound solitude and silence they performed their rites. They began by bathing the tomb with their tears, after which they laid an olive branch and a laurel crown upon it, and deposited the carved stone at its foot. Finally one of those present broke silence by pronouncing, with great emotion, an address to Rousseau, which began with the words 'Rousseau, ombre chère et sacrée', and proceeded in similar vein at some length.

The ceremony being over, they settled down to meditate round the tomb, each at the foot of a poplar, and to seek inspiration from Rousseau's spiritual presence. One tried to compose music after the style of the *Devin du Village*, another sketched the tomb, a third simply 'poured on to the paper the wonderful thoughts which came into his head'. Suddenly, however, they felt themselves seized by some strange and unknown power. Their pens fell to the ground and a voice, which they immediately recognized as the voice of Rousseau, was heard from the depths of the tomb, distinctly pronouncing these words: 'Nation généreuse et sensible! Braves Français! Citoyens compatriotes! Amis!' In a style remarkably adapted to the conventions of revolutionary oratory, Rousseau's voice continued to tell them that they had justified the confidence he had placed in them, and by doing so, had amply repaid him for the persecution he had endured on their account. He congratulated them on the constitution, which followed so closely the path he had traced for them; he instructed them to forgive his enemies, sent messages of congratulation to an assortment of members of the Assembly, and asked them to correct Mme. de Staël's erroneous statement that he had taken his own life. His disciples listened in wonder and terror, and returned to Paris in exalted spirits to tell the world of their experience.[1]

Such expressions of the revolutionary cult of Rousseau

[1] *Prosopopée de J. J. Rousseau*, etc., 1791. Mention of this incident is also made by Ginguené in his *Letters on the Confessions of J. J. Rousseau*, p. 3.

indicate a very real feeling of being spiritually at one with Rousseau, a feeling which was none the less sincere for all their ignorance of Rousseau's political theory, and for all the misinterpretations of that political theory which the Revolution set on foot. The aristocratic accusation that the revolutionaries deliberately and consciously misinterpreted Rousseau's political ideas was an over-simplification. Their enthusiasm was based, not on his political writings, but on the Rousseauist myth which the Revolution took over from the pre-revolutionary cult, and according to which Rousseau featured as a great moralist, whose work in directing the attention of the individual to his moral rights and duties was a necessary prerequisite to the achievements of 1789.

The third element in Professor McNeil's analysis is also, it seems to me, invalidated by more detailed study. He argues that the revolutionary cult of Rousseau was unable to achieve an independent existence because it was merely used to bolster up the views of first this, then that political faction. It would be more accurate to describe the Rousseauist cult as having so general, and at the same time so intensely personal a hold upon the minds of the revolutionary generation that the ideas associated with Rousseau's name retained their significance for each succeeding faction as well as for countless individuals, both revolutionary and anti-revolutionary. The personal and moral appeal of the Rousseauist cult survived into the Revolution, and the general political principles which were grafted on to it were sufficiently general to be acceptable to all those who had set themselves the task of regenerating French society, and who regarded Rousseau's name as one of the most important symbols of their hopes. Thus the individual and at the same time universal character of the Rousseauist cult ensured its continued survival, and it is possible to find at every stage in the Revolution both an official cult of Rousseau and at the same time individuals who appealed to his name, whether they belonged to the predominant faction or whether they opposed it, whether they defended or whether they attacked the Revolution itself. Those who disagreed with the particular faction in power as to the methods which should be used to push forward or to conserve the Revolution, still accepted the common inspiration and the common purpose of the Revolution which they regarded Rousseau as having stated. Those who feared the Revolution and opposed it still appealed to the great thinker who had formed the minds of their generation.

In the course of this study something has already been shown of the loyalty felt to Rousseau's memory by opposing factions. During the very years when Rousseau's name was coming to be increasingly venerated as a revolutionary symbol, during the period which culminated in the National Assembly's decree of December 1790, when official recognition was given for Rousseau's supposed contribution to the Revolution, other writers and politicians were appealing passionately to the authority of Rousseau to condemn the very Revolution with which his name had become so closely associated. It has been shown that in fact these aristocratic writers were the most scholarly exponents of Rousseau's political theory, but this achievement on their part was very largely accidental. Adherents of the personal and literary cult of Rousseau, they were shocked to find the name of a man whose memory they held in such esteem, being used to justify political measures which they could not condone. As Lenormant and Ferrand explicitly admitted, they were drawn to examine the *Social Contract* in detail because of the way in which the revolutionaries had appropriated Rousseau's name to support policies of which they did not approve.[1] The revolutionaries, on the contrary, being convinced of their spiritual alignment with one whom they had adopted as their great precursor, had less incentive to make an objective and critical study of Rousseau's political theory, and were obviously not inclined to emphasize those points at which Rousseau's theory parted company with the accepted conventions of the Revolution. Yet it is important to remember that both revolutionaries and aristocrats appealed to the authority of Rousseau in the first place not because of his political writings, but because the Rousseauist myth had become an integral part of the common intellectual background of the educated classes.

This study of the influence and interpretation of Rousseau's political theory extends only as far as 1791, but there are indications that the same pattern continued through the

[1] See Ch. IX.

revolutionary period. There continued to be an official association between the group in power and the cult of Rousseau on the one hand, while on the other, individuals still continued to appeal to Rousseau's authority both to support and to oppose the ruling faction. For example, Robespierre has probably been credited with having been inspired by Rousseau's works more than any other revolutionary leader. Both he and Saint-Just were admirers of Rousseau, and the members of the Committee of Public Safety frequently quoted Rousseau's name. Yet we know that among the opponents of the Jacobins there were admirers of Rousseau as ardent and sincere as Robespierre and Saint-Just. Mme. Roland, we have seen, constantly expressed her admiration for him in her letters and claimed that the reading of the *Nouvelle Héloise* was a turning point in her life.[1] Buzot in flight from his enemies, regretted the time when he had wandered among the fields of Normandy with a volume of Rousseau's works in his hands.[2] Louvet, hiding from his enemies in the Jura, wrote:

> Alors, je me rappelle que ce fut ton sort, O mon maître, O mon soutien sublime et vertueux Rousseau. Toi aussi, pour avoir bien merité du genre humain, tu t'en vis persécuté. Toi aussi, pour avoir été l'ami du peuple. . . .[3]

Similarly, when Robespierre was overthrown, the revolutionary cults, including that of Rousseau, were stronger under the Directory than at any time during the Revolution.[4] The President of the Executive was La Revellière-Lépeaux, who has already been mentioned as an ardent admirer of Rousseau.[5] At the same time, Babeuf, executed under the Directory, was also a fervent Rousseauist, who christened his son 'Émile'. Babeuf numbered among his associates Sylvain Maréchal, who has already been noted as a contributor to the Rousseauist journal *Révolutions de Paris*, and the instigator, in 1790, of a fund for the erection of a statue to Rousseau.[6]

[1] *Vie Privée*, *Œuvres*, I, 207.
[2] *Mémoires sur la Révolution française*, ed. Guadet, 1928.
[3] *Quelques notices pour l'histoire et le récit de mes périls, depuis le 31 Mai, 1793*, p. 182.
[4] Mathiez, *Les Origines des cultes*, etc.
[5] See above, p. 48, nn. 1, 2.
[6] See above, p. 157, n. 6.

Thus it is possible to find at every stage in the Revolution individuals in practically every faction who appealed to Rousseau's authority, and who were familiar with and admired his works. For this reason the revolutionary cult cannot be regarded as an artificial phenomenon, officially cultivated by the successive factions which acquired transitory dominance. On the contrary, its continued existence and its personal attraction for so many of such diverse opinions is evidence of the power which the Rousseauist myth continued to exercise over the minds of the revolutionary generation. The diversity of viewpoint among those who appealed to Rousseau's authority helps to explain why historians have reached such a variety of conclusions about his political influence. Such general conclusions, however, ignore the distinction between individual loyalty to Rousseau's memory, which was the fundamental basis of the official cult, and the actual knowledge and application of Rousseau's political theory, as stated in the *Social Contract*. Of the men of the revolutionary generation one might say that all of them and at the same time none of them were Rousseauists, in that while the literary and personal cult of Rousseau had become an integral part of their intellectual equipment, those who read the *Social Contract* and accepted its specific theories were a mere handful. In every revolutionary faction there were admirers of Rousseau; in every argument between those in power and those in opposition, appeal was apt to be made at some stage and by individuals on both sides to Rousseau's authority. But this appeal to Rousseau's name had not necessarily any connection with his political writings, of which, at least during the period 1789–91, the majority of the protagonists were very largely ignorant.

Since Rousseau's name had been most intimately associated with that gospel of regeneration which the revolutionaries were supposed to be putting into practice, it was natural, if illogical, on the part of the revolutionaries to suppose that Rousseau would have approved the means which they used to achieve the ends which he stated. It was equally natural, if also illogical, that they should have cherished a deep respect for the work in which Rousseau's political theory had been enshrined, particularly since its publication had played so important a part in the history of Rousseau's 'martyrdom', an essential component of the Rousseauist cult. Thus the actual contents of the *Social Contract* were for a very large number of people immaterial; the *Social Contract* itself was part of the myth, and it was the myth of Rousseau rather than his political theory which was important in the mind of the revolutionary generation.

BIBLIOGRAPHY

I. Contemporary Sources

1. *Works of Rousseau*

Political Works of Rousseau, ed. C. E. Vaughan, Cambridge, 1915, Vols. I, II.

Correspondance Générale, ed. T. Dufour, Paris, 1924–1934.

La Nouvelle Héloise, ed. D. Mornet, Paris, 1927. Vols. I–IV.

Œuvres Complètes de J. J. Rousseau, ed. L. S. Mercier, G. Brizzard, F. H. S. de l'Aulnaye, Paris, 1788–93. Vols. I–XXXVIII.

2. *Other Eighteenth Century Political Theorists*

BONNOT DE MABLY, G., *De l'Étude de l'histoire*, Parma, 1775.

——, *De la législation, ou principes des lois*, Paris, 1777.

DIDEROT, D., *Œuvres complètes*, ed. J. Assézat, M. Tourneux, Paris, 1875–7.

GRAVINA, J. V., *L'Esprit des lois romaines*, tr. J. B. Requier, Paris, 1776.

HELVÉTIUS, C. O., *De l'Esprit*, Paris, 1758. *De l'Homme*, London, 1773.

D'HOLBACH, P. H. D. (Baron), *Système de la Nature*, Paris, 1821.

MORELLY, *Code de la Nature*, ed. É. Dolléans, Paris, 1910.

PUFENDORF, S. (Baron), *Le droit de la nature et des gens*, etc., tr. J. Barbeyrac, Amsterdam, 1712.

SECONDAT, C. L. DE (Baron Montesquieu), *De L'Esprit des lois*, ed. P. Janet, Paris, 1892.

3. *Studies of Rousseau and the Social Contract*

BARÈRE, B., *Éloge de J. J. Rousseau, citoyen de Genève*, 1788. [*B.N. Ln. 1. 28.*]

BARRUEL-BEAUVERT, A. J. DE (Comte), *Vie de J. J. Rousseau*, 1789. [*B.M. 275. 9. 2.*]

BEAUCLAIR, J. P. L. DE, *L'Anti Contrat Social*, 1764. [*B.M. 1103a. 16.*]

BERTHIER, G. F., *Observations sur le Contrat Social de J. J. Rousseau*, 1789. (Written in 1762.)

BILHON, J. F., *Éloge de J. J. Rousseau*, 1788. [*B.N. Ln. 27. 17976.*]

BOUILLY, J., *J. J. Rousseau à ses derniers moments*, 1790. (Performed at the Théâtre des Italiens in December of that year.)

CERUTTI, J. A. J., 'Lettres sur quelques passages des Confessions', *Journal de Paris*, 2 December 1789, Vol. II, Supplement No. 333.

CHAMPCENETZ, L. DE (Marquis), *Réponse aux lettres sur le caractère et les ouvrages de J. J. Rousseau*, etc., *1789*. [*B.M. 11805 cc. 346.*]

DAUNOU, P. C. F., 'De la religion publique, ou Réflexions sur un chapitre du Contrat Social de J. J. Rousseau', *L'Esprit des Journaux*, April 1790, p. 222 ff. (Reprinted from *Journal Encyclopédique*.)

DELORTHE, G. A., *Éloge de J. J. Rousseau*, 1790. [*BN. Ln. 27. 17955.*]

D'ESCHERNY, F. L. (Comte), *De l'influence de J. J. Rousseau sur la Révolution présente*, 1791. [*BN. Lb. 39. 4812.*]

——, *Éloge de J. J. Rousseau*, 1790. [*BM. 1088f. 29. 34.*]

D'EYMAR, A. M., BARÈRE, B. and others, *Recueil des pièces relatives à la motion faite à l'Assemblée Nationale au sujet de J. J. Rousseau et de sa veuve*, 1791. [*BM. FR. 371.*]

GINGUENÉ, P. L., *Letters on the confessions of J. J. Rousseau* (tr. unknown), London, 1792. [*BM.* 631. *d. 36.*]

GINGUENÉ, P. L., MERCIER, L. S. and others, i. *Pétition à l'Assemblée Nationale contenant demande de la translation des cendres de J. J. Rousseau au Panthéon français*. ii. *Pétition des citoyens de la ville et du canton de Montmorency à l'Assemblée Nationale*. iii. *Réponse de M. le Président de l'Assemblée Nationale, Vte. de Broglie*, 1791. [*BN. Le. 29. 1731.*]

GRÉGOIRE, H. B. (Abbé), *Éloge de J. J. Rousseau*, 1791. [*BN. Ln. 27. 17984.*]

GUDIN, P. P., *Supplément au Contrat Social applicable particulièrement aux grandes nations*, 1790. [*BM. 8277 d. 40.*]

LEGROS, J. C. F. (Abbé), *Analyse des ouvrages de J. J. Rousseau de Genève et de M. Court de Gebelin, par un solitaire*, 1785. [*BM. 11826 cc. 18.*]

LENORMANT, C. F. (Comte), *J. J. Rousseau, Aristocrate*, 1790. [*BM. F. 374.*]

LUZAC, É., *Lettre d'un Anonyme*, 1776. See Derathé, *Annales*, 1950. Vol. 32.

MEUDE-MONPAS, J. J. O., *Éloge de J. J. Rousseau*, 1791. [*BM. F. 1088.*]

MERCIER, L. S., *J. J. Rousseau considéré comme l'un des premiers auteurs de la Révolution*, 1791. [*BM. 631. G. 8.*]

NAVILLE, P., *Examen du Contrat Social de J. J. Rousseau (1762), publié d'après le manuscrit autographe*. See Fabre, *Annales*, 1933, Vol. XXII.

PARIS, DE L'ORATOIRE, 'Hommage de la Nation à J. J. Rousseau', *Mercure de France*, 12 February 1791. No. 7, p. 49 ff.

STAËL HOLSTEIN, A. (Baronne), *Lettres sur les ouvrages et le caractère de J. J. Rousseau*, 1789. [*BM. R. 407.*]

THIERY, L., *Éloge de J. J. Rousseau*, 1791. [*BM. F. 1093. 13.*]

4. *Political Pamphlets, Articles and Speeches*

LAUNAY D'ANTRAIGUES, E. L. H., DE (Comte), *Discours d'un membre de l'Assemblée Nationale à ses co-députés*, 1789. [*BM. E. 1001. 2. 3.*]

——, *Discours prononcé . . . à l'Assemblée des députés des trois ordres de la Province de Languedoc*, 1789. [*BM. 910. C. 14 (1–37).*]

——, *Discours prononcé . . . aux États Généraux dans la Chambre de la Noblesse*, 1789. [*Ibid.*]

——, *Discours prononcé dans la Chambre de la Noblesse*, 1789. [*BM. F. 90 (1–15).*]

——, *Mémoire sur la vérification des pouvoirs, lue à la première conférence chez M. le Gardes-des-Sceaux, 1789*. [*BM. 910. C. 14 (1–37).*]

——, *Mémoire sur les États Généraux, leurs droits et la manière de les convoquer*, 1788. [*BM. 282. d. 6.*]

LAUNAY D'ANTRAIGUES, E. L. H., DE (*cont.*), *Mémoire sur les Mandats Impératifs*, 1789. [*BM. FR. 50. 1. 43.*]
——, *Première motion de M. M. les Commissaires conciliateurs de l'Ordre de la Noblesse*, 1789. [*BM. 910. C. 14 (1–37).*]
——, *Quelle est la situation de l'Assemblée Nationale?*, 1790. [*BM. FR. 53.*]
——, *Second Discours d'un Membre de l'Assemblée Nationale à ses co-députés*, 1789. [*BM. F. 1001. 2. 3.*]
BERGASSE, N., *Discours sur la manière dont il convient de limiter le pouvoir législatif et le pouvoir exécutif dans une monarchie*, 1790. [*BM. FR. 76 (2).*]
BILLAUD-VARENNE, J. N., *L'Acéphocratie, ou le gouvernement fédératif démontré le meilleur pour un grand empire*, 1791. [*BN. Lb. 39. 10087.*]
——, *Discours sur les émigrations*, 1791. [*BM. F. 338. 9.*]
BOURDEILLE, C. DE, *Réflexions sur les affaires politiques du temps présent de la France*, 1790. [*BN. Lb. 39. 3565.*]
BRISSOT, J. P., *Discours sur les Conventions*, 1791. [*BM. 347. 8.*]
——, *Plan de conduite pour les députés du peuple aux États Généraux de 1789*, 1789. [*BM. F. 670.*]
CALONNE, C. A. DE, *De l'état de France présent et à venir*, 1790. [*BN. Lb. 39. 4. 294.*]
CLERMONT-TONNERRE, S. DE (Comte), *Sur le droit que le Monarque doit avoir sur la nomination des juges*, 1790. [*BN. Le. 39. 626. 664.*]
DAUNOU, P. C. F., *Le Contrat Social des Français*, 1789. [*BM. F. 27–28.*]
DEMAREST, — *Coup d'oeil rapide et impartiel sur les opinions du jour*, 1790. [*BM. R. 200.*]
DUCREST, C. L. (Marquis), *Essai sur les principes d'une bonne constitution*, 1789. [*BM. F. 18. 20.*]
ÉLMOTHE, P. D', *Épître à J. J. Rousseau, Mercure de France*, January 1790.
FAUCHET, C. (Abbé), 'Discours sur le Contrat Social de J. J. Rousseau', *Bouche de Fer*, October 1790 to April 1791, Nos. XI–XXXXI.
——, *Encore quatre cris d'un patriote*, 1789. [*BM. R. 360.*]
——, *La Religion Nationale*, 1789. [*BM. R. 164.*]
——, *Seconde motion . . . sur les droits des représentants et du peuple*, 1789. [*Ibid.*]
——, *Troisième discours sur la liberté française, 1759.* [*BM. F. 245–6–7.*]
FERRAND, A. F. C. DE (Comte), *Adresse d'un citoyen très-actif*, 1789. [*BN. Lb. 39. 2717.*]
——, *Le dernier coup de la ligue*, 1790. [*BM. F. 23. 24.*]
——, *Nullité et despotisme de l'Assemblée Nationale, 1790.* [*BM. R. 72.*]
ISNARD, A. N., *Observations sur le principe qui a produit les révolutions de France, de Genève et d'Amérique, dans le dix-huitième siècle*, 1789. [*BM. R. 193.*]
MALOUET, P. V. (Baron), *Lettre à ses commettans*, 1789. [*BM. F. 66.*]
——, *Lettre à ses commettans*, 1790. [*BM. F. 1520 (2).*]
——, *Motion sur le discours adressé par le roi à l'Assemblée Nationale*, 1790. [*BM. F. 926 (11).*]
——, *Opinion sur l'acte constitutionnel commencée et interrompue dans la séance du 8 Août*, 1791. [*BM. FR. 76.*]
——, *Opinion sur la sanction royale*, 1789. [*BM. F. 68.***]
——, *Opinion sur le projet de décret contre les protestations*, 1791. [*BM. R. 81.*]

MANDAR, T., *De la souveraineté du peuple et de l'excellence d'un état libre, par Marchemont Needham, traduit de l'Anglais et enrichi de notes de J. J. Rousseau, Mably, Condillac, Montesquieu, Letrosne, Raynal, etc.*, 1790. [*BN. E. 4947.*]

MAURY, J. S. (Abbé), *Opinion sur la souveraineté du peuple*, 1790. [*BN. Le. 29. 1919.*]

——, *Réplique . . . sur le droit qui appartient au roi de choisir et d'instituer les juges*, 1790. [*BN. Le. 29. 626–664.*]

MOUNIER, J., *Considérations sur les gouvernements, et principalement celui qui convient à la France*, 1789. [*BM. 910. C. 15.*]

PÉTION, J., *Opinion sur l'appel au peuple*, 1789. [*BM. FR. 76.*]

PROUST, J., *Le triomphe de la philosophie, ou la réception de Voltaire et de J. J. Rousseau aux Champs Elysées; Fête célébrée à Angers*, 1789. [*BM. 911. 64.*]

RÉAL, P. F., *Opinion sur la question de savoir quel parti il faut prendre dans les circonstances actuelles*, 1791. [*BM. F. 343. 4.*]

ROBERT, F., *Le républicanisme adapté à la France*, 1790. [*BM. FR. 76.*]

ROBESPIERRE, M., *Dire . . . contre le véto royal*, 1789, *Discours*, Vol. VI, p. 86.

——, *Discours sur les États de Cambrésis*, 1789, *Ibid.*, p. 143 ff.

——, *Sur l'inviolabilité des représentants*, 1790. *Ibid.*, p. 429 ff.

ROUSSET, S., *L'Ombre de Voltaire et de J. J. Rousseau aux Champs Elysées, rencontre de ces deux grands hommes*, etc., 1791. [*BN. La. 2720808.*]

SERVAN, A. J. M., *Essai sur la formation des assemblées nationales, provinciales et municipales*, 1789. [*BM. R. 72.*]

SÈZE, R. DE (Comte), *Opinion sur la sanction royale*, 1789. [*BM. RF. 76.*]

SIEYES, E. J. DE (Abbé), *Préliminaire de la constitution*, 1789. [*BM. F. 797–8.*]

——, *Qu'est-ce que le Tiers État?* 1789. ed. E. Champion, Paris, 1888.

——, *Sur la question du véto royal*, 1789. [*BM. F. 27–28.*]

SIMONNE, J. C., *Discours sur la loi à faire contre les émigrations*, 1791. [*BM. F. 336. 7.*]

TALLEYRAND-PERIGORD, C. M. DE, *Motion sur les Mandats impératifs*, 1789. [*BM. F. 789.*]

VACHARD, —, *Installation de J. J. Rousseau, auteur du Contrat Social, dans la société des Indigens, amis de la Constitution*, 1791. [*BM. F. 340. 1. 2.*]

AUBERT DE VITRY, F. J., *J. J. Rousseau à l'Assemblée Nationale*, 1789. [*BM. R. 407.*]

ANONYMOUS

Adresse à tous les membres, soit en corps, soit séparément, des trois ordres de l'Empire français . . . contre les auteurs du système républicain connu et annoncé sous le titre de création de deux chambres, etc., 1791. [*BM. FR. 76.*]

Adresse aux Français de toutes classes, victimes de la Révolution, 1790. [*BN. Lb. 39. 3564.*]

Adresse de la Société des Amis de la Constitution aux sociétés qui lui sont affiliées, 1791. [*BM. F. 333. 4. 5.*]

À l'Assemblée prétendue nationale, 1790. [*BM. R. 76.*]

Apologie de la noblesse de France par l'auteur de l'Adresse au Roi, réfugié à Madrid, 1790. [*L.A. 8H. 9. 653.*]

Catéchisme anti-constitutionnel, ou sentiments de Solon, Tacite, Gordon, Sidney, Locke, J. J. Rousseau, etc., sur ce qui s'est passé et se passera en 1789 et 1790, 1790. [*BN. Lb. 39. 3273.*]

De la nécessité de montrer à la nation . . . le bon et le mauvais des travaux de ses députés, 1790. [*BM. R. 76.*]

De l'autorité de Montesquieu dans la Révolution présente, 1789. (Attributed by Monglond to P. A. Grouvelle.) [*BM. R. 198.*]

De J. J. Rousseau, du Parlement et de M. Necker, par un ancien militaire bon patriote, 1789. [*BN. Ln. 27. 17987.*]

Dictionnaire social et patriotique, Paris, 1770.

Examen impartiel de cette question: comment et dans quelle forme doit-on procéder aux délibérations? 1789. [*BM. F. 23–24.*]

Fête champêtre célébrée à Montmorency en l'honneur de J. J. Rousseau, 1790. [*BN. Lb. 40. 1004.*]

Jean-Jacques, ou le Réveil-Matin des représentants de la nation française, 1789. [*BM. R. 193.*]

J. J. Rousseau dans l'Isle de Saint-Pierre. (Performed in Paris at the Théâtre de la Nation in December 1791.) See *Mercure de France*, 14 January 1792, p. 57.

J. J. Rousseau des Champs Elysées à la nation française, 1789. [*BM. R. 40.*]

'L'Assemblée National', see *L'Année Littéraire*, 1789, Vol. VIII, Lettres, VII, XVII.

La décadence de l'Empire français fruit de la philosophie moderne adaptée par nos législateurs, 1790. [*BN. Lb. 39. 3359.*]

La monarchie vengée des attentats des républicains modernes, 1791. [*La. H. 9642 (1).*]

L'Abus des mots, 1790. [*BM. R. 198.*]

Le dernier cri de la vérité sur la Révolution française, 1791. [*LA. 8H. 9485.*]

Le despotisme décreté par l'Assemblée Nationale. [*BM. R. 72.*]

Le disciple de Montesquieu à M.M. les députés aux États Généraux, 1789. [*BM. FR. 18.*]

Le naviget anticyras, ou le système sans principe, l'édifice sans fondement, élevé sur le sable, 1790. [*BM. R. 197.*]

Le quatorze juillet, 1790, ou fédération de la ligue contre Louis XVI, 1790. [*LA. 8H. 9485. 4.*]

Le réveil des rois, ou essai sur la fausseté des principes des démocrates actuels, sur la Révolution de France, etc., 1791. [*BN. L. 39. 4485.*]

Les États Généraux convoqués par Louis XVI, 1789. [*BM. R. 52.*]

Les Sabats Jacobites, 1791, Nos. 1–75. [*BN. F. 1571. 2. 3.*]

'Le tableau de rapprochement: les principes et les effets de la constitution française.' See *Actes des Apôtres*, 1790. Intro. Series V.

Lettre de J. J. Rousseau à l'Assemblée Nationale, No. 1, Des Champs Elysées, l'an 5793, 1789. [*BN. Lb. 39. 2328.*]

Lettre d'un impartiel à un anonyme, 1790. [*BM. R. 193.*]

Lettres à quelques propriétaires, 1789. [*BM. FR. 44.*]

Lisez ceci bons Français, 1790. [*LA. 8. H. 9485. 4.*]

Motion d'un campagnard curé de village, sur la Déclaration des droits, 1789. [*BM. FR. 76.*]

Première lettre à M. de la Cretelle, 1788. [*BM. R. 50.*]

Prosopopée de J. J. Rousseau, ou sentiments de reconnaissance des amis de l'Institution d'Émile à l'Assemblée Nationale . . . à l'occasion de son décret de 21 Decembre 1790, 1790. [*BM. FR. 371. 1–49.*]

Qui est-ce donc qui gagne à la Révolution? 1790. [*BN. Lb. 39. 3160.*]

'Sophismes politiques'. See *Actes des Apôtres*, 1790. No. 52.

Théorie des États Généraux, ou la France régénérée, 1769. [*BM. FR. 18.*]

5. *Journals*

Les Actes des Apôtres, November 1789–October 1791, Vols. I–X.

L'Année Littéraire, January 1789–May 1790.

La Bouche de Fer, October 1789–July 1791, Vols. I, II.

Le Courrier de Provence, May 1789–September 1791, Vols. I–XVII.

L'Esprit des Journaux, January 1789–December 1791, Vols. I–XXXVI.

Le Journal des débats de la Société des Amis de la Constitution, June–December 1791, Nos. 1–20.

Journal de Paris, January 1789–December 1791, Vols. I–VI.

Mercure britannique, 1798–1800, Vols. I–V.

Mercure de France, January 1789–December 1791, Vols. I–XXXVI.

Réimpression de l'Ancien Moniteur, Paris, 1858, Vols. I–IV.

Révolutions de Paris, September 1789–December 1791, Vols. I–VII.

Les Sabats Jacobites (Issues undated), 1791, Vols. I, II, Nos. 1–75.

6. *Memoirs*

BARÈRE, B., *Mémoires*, ed. H. Carnot, Paris, 1842.

BRISSOT, J. P., *Mémoires, 1754–93*, ed. C. Perroud, Paris, 1910.

BRIZZARD, G. (Abbé), *Pélerinage à Ermenonville aux Mânes de J. J. Rousseau*, 1783. (M.S.). [*L.A. Fol. 331.*]

DUMONT, É., 'Rousseau, jugé par Étienne Dumont: Pages oubliées et inédites'; Louis Courtois: *Annales*, 1933, Vol. XXII.

——, *Souvenirs sur Mirabeau*, ed. Bénétruy, Paris, 1951.

D'ESCHERNY, F. L. (Comte), *De J. J. Rousseau et des philosophes du 18ᵉ siècle: Mélanges de Littérature*, etc. Paris, 1811, Vol. III.

GIRARDIN, S. DE, *Discours et Opinions, Journal et Souvenirs*, Paris, 1828, Vols. I–IV.

GRÉGOIRE, H. B. (Comte, Évêque constitutionnel de Blois), *Mémoires*, ed. H. Carnot, Paris, 1837, Vols. I, II.

LIGNE, CH. DE (Prince), *Letters and Memoirs*, ed. L. Ashton, London, 1927.

LOUVET, J. B., *Mémoires sur la Révolution française*, ed. F. Aulard, Paris, 1889. Vols. I, II. *Quelques notices pour l'histoire et le récit de mes périls depuis le 31 Mai 1793*, Paris, l'an III.

METRA, F. (etc.), *Correspondance secrète, politique et littéraire*, Paris, 1789, etc.

MOUNIER, J. J., *On the influence attributed to philosophers, freemasons, etc., on the Revolution of France*, tr. J. Walker, London, 1801.

OESLNER, C., *Notice sur la vie de Sieyes*, Paris, 1796. [*BN. Ln. 27. 1896.*]

PHILIPON ROLAND, M. J., *Lettres de Mme Roland aux Demoiselles Cannet*, etc., ed. C. A. Dauban, Paris, 1867. Vols. I, II.

——, *Vie Privée*, Paris, l'an VIII. Vols. I, II.

LA REVELLIÈRE-LÉPEAUX, L. M., *Mémoires*, ed. D. d'Angers, Paris, 1895, Vols. I–III.

II. Secondary Sources

1. *Studies of Rousseau*

BALDENSPERGER, F. and others, *J. J. Rousseau: Leçons faites à l'École des Hautes Études Sociales*, Paris, 1912.

BUFFENOIR, H., *Les portraits de J. J. Rousseau*, Paris, 1905.

——, *Le prestige de J. J. Rousseau*, Paris, 1909.

CAHEN, R., 'Rousseau et la Révolution francaise', *Revue de Paris*, 1912, Ann. XIX.

CHAMPION, E., *Rousseau et la Révolution française*, Paris, 1909.

CHUQUOT, A., *Jean-Jacques Rousseau*, Paris, 1906.

COBBAN, A., *Rousseau and the Modern State*, London, 1964.

COLE, G. D. H., *The Social Contract and Discourses of J. J. Rousseau*, London, 1941.

DERATHÉ, R., *J. J. Rousseau et la science politique de son temps*, Paris, 1950.

——, *Le rationalisme de J. J. Rousseau*, Paris, 1948.

——, 'Les réfutations du Contrat Social au dix-huitième siècle', *Annales*, Vol. 32 (1950).

FABRE, J., *Jean-Jacques Rousseau*, Paris, 1912.

FAGUET, E., *Rousseau, penseur*, Paris, 1910.

GREEN, F. C., *J. J. Rousseau*, London, 1955.

HENDEL, C., *J. J. Rousseau, Moralist*, London and New York, 1934.

LEMAÎTRE, J., *Jean-Jacques Rousseau*, tr. J. Mairet and Mme. C. Bigot, London, 1908.

LÉON, P.-L., 'L'idée de volonté générale chez J. J. Rousseau et ses antécédents historiques,' *Archives de Philosophie du droit et de sociologie juridique*, (1936), Nos. 3–4.

MCNEIL, G., 'The Anti-Revolutionary Rousseau,' *American History Review*, Vol. LVIII (1952–3), pp. 808–23.

——, 'The Cult of Rousseau and the French Revolution,' *Journal of the History of Ideas*, Vol. VI, (April 1945), No. 2, pp. 197–212.

MADAY, A. DE, 'Rousseau et la Révolution,' *Annales*, Vol. XXI, (1937).

MEYNIER, A., *J. J. Rousseau, révolutionnaire*, Paris, 1911.

MORNET, D., 'L'influence de J. J. Rousseau au xviiie siècle,' *Annales*, Vol. XIX (1912).

——, 'Les Éditions de la Nouvelle Héloise,' *Annales*, Vol. V, (1909).

——, *Le sentiment de la nature en France de J. J. Rousseau à Bernardin de Saint-Pierre: Essai sur les rapports de la littérature et des moeurs*, Paris, 1907.

——, *Rousseau, l'homme et l'oeuvre*, Paris, 1950.

MOWAT, R. B., *Jean-Jacques Rousseau*, London, 1938.

PLAN, P.-P., *J. J. Rousseau raconté par les gazettes de son temps*, Paris, 1912.

SCHINZ, A., *La pensée de J. J. Rousseau*, Paris, 1929.

WILLIAMS, D., 'The influence of Rousseau on political opinion, 1760–95,' *English Historical Review*, XLVIII (1933), pp. 414–30. (See also *Annales*, XX for a review of this article.)

2. *General Histories*

AULARD, F. A., *Histoire politique de la Révolution, 1789–1104*, Paris, 1901.

——, *Les Orateurs de la Révolution: L'Assemblée constituante*, Paris, 1905; *La Société des Jacobins*, Paris, 1889–97.

BASTID, P., *Sieyes et sa pensée*, Paris, 1939.

BAYET, A. and ALBERT, F., *Écrivains politiques du XVIIIe siècle*, Paris, 1907.

BECKER, C., *The Heavenly City of the eighteenth century philosophers*, New York, 1932.

BELIN, J., *La logique d'une idée-force: l'idée d'utilité sociale et la Révolution française, 1789–92*, Paris, 1939.

BICKART, R., *Les Parlements et la notion de souveraineté nationale au XVIIIe siècle*, Paris, 1932.

BLANC, L., *Histoire de la Révolution française*, Paris, 1866.

BRADBY, E. D., *Short History of the French Revolution*, London, 1926.

CHARRIER, J., *Claude Fauchet, Évêque constitutionnel de Calvados*, Paris, 1909.

COBBAN, A., 'The Parlements of France in the eighteenth century.' *History*, Vol. XXXV (1950), pp. 64–80.

VAN DEUSEN, G., *Sieyes, his life and nationalism*, Paris, 1933.

GARRETT, M. B., *The Estates General of 1789*, New York and London, 1935.

KOUNG, Y., *Théorie constitutionnelle de Sieyes*, Paris, 1934.

LEFEBVRE, G., *The coming of the French Revolution*, tr. R. R. Palmer, Princeton University Press, 1947.

LEMAIRE, A., *Les lois fondamentales de la Monarchie française*, Paris, 1907.

LEROY, M., *Histoire des idées sociales en France, de Montesquieu à Robespierre*, Paris, 1946.

MATHIEZ, A., *Les Origines des cultes révolutionnaires*, Paris, 1904.

——, *La Révolution française*, Paris, 1922–7.

——, 'La Révolution française et la théorie de la dictature,' *Revue Historique*, July–August 1929.

MEYNIER, A., *Un représentant de la bourgeoisie angevine: La Revellière-Lépeaux*, Paris, 1905.

MICHELET, J., *Histoire de la Révolution française*, Paris, 1868.

MORNET, D., 'Les enseignements des bibliothèques privées, 1750-80,' *Revue de l'histoire littéraire de la France*, Vol. XVII (1910), pp. 449–95. (See also *Annales*, VI (1910), for a review of this study.)

——, *Les origines intellectuelles de la Révolution française*, Paris, 1933.

PINGAUD, L., *Un agent secret sous la Révolution et l'Empire: Le comte d'Antraigues*, Paris, 1894.

QUINET, E., *La Révolution*, Paris, 1866.

ROCQUAIN, F., *L'esprit révolutionnaire avant la Révolution*, Paris, 1878.

SAINTE BEUVE C. A., *Causeries du Lundi*, 1851, Vol. v. See E. de Beauverger, 'Étude sur Sieyes.'

TAINE, H., *Les Origines de la France contemporaine*, Paris, 1875. See Vol. I, *L'Ancien Régime*,

TALMON, J. L., *The Origins of totalitarian democracy*, London, 1952.

THOMPSON, E., *Popular sovereignty and the French Constituent Assembly, 1789–91*, Manchester, 1952.

TRAHARD, P., *La sensibilité révolutionnaire*, Paris, 1936.

3. *Works of Reference*

ARNAULT, A. V. and others, *Biographie nouvelle des contemporains*, Paris, 1820–5. 20 vols.

BARBIER, A. A., *Dictionnaire des ouvrages anonymes*, Paris, 1806–8. 4 vols.

——, *Notice des principaux écrits relatifs à la personne et aux ouvrages de J. J. Rousseau*, Paris, 1818.

BOULOISEAU, M., LEFEBVRE, G. and SOBOUL, A., *Oeuvres complètes de Robespierre: Discours, 1789–91*, Paris, 1950, Vol. VI.

DUFOUR, T. and PLAN, P.-P., *Recherches bibliographiques sur J. J. Rousseau*, Paris, 1925.

FLAMMERONT, J., *Remontrances du Parlement de Paris au XVIIIe siècle*, Paris, 1888–98. 3 vols.

HATIN, E., *Bibliographie historique et critique de la presse périodique française*, Paris, 1866.

LANSON, G., *Manuel bibliographique de la littérature française moderne*, Paris, 1925.

MONGLOND, A., *La France révolutionnaire et impériale*, Grenoble, 1930–5. 8 vols.

QUÉRARD, J., *La France littéraire*, Paris, 1827–39. 12 vols.

ROBINET, J., *Dictionnaire historique et biographique de la Révolution*, Paris, 1899. 2 vols.

SCHINZ, A. *État présent des travaux sur J. J. Rousseau*, Baltimore, 1941.

SENÉLIER, J., *Bibliographie générale des Oeuvres de J. J. Rousseau*, Paris, 1948.

TOURNEUX, M., *Bibliographie de l'histoire de Paris pendant la Révolution française*, Paris, 1890–1906. 5 vols.

TUETEY, T., *Répertoire général des sources manuscrites de l'histoire de Paris pendant la Révolution française*, Paris, 1890–1912. 10 vols.

Journal des Débats et des Décrets: Assemblée Nationale Constituante, 17th June 1789–20th September 1791, No. 1–862.

Procès-Verbal de l'Assemblée des Communes et de l'Assemblée Nationale, June 1789–20 September 1791.

Procès-Verbal des Conférences sur la vérification des pouvoirs, 1789.

INDEX

McDonald, J.
Rousseau and the French Revolution, 1762-1791.